A QUICK COURSE IN

WINDOWS

Version 3

SALLEY OBERLIN

PATRICK KERVRAN

PUBLISHED BY
Online Press Incorporated
14320 NE 21st Street, Suite 18
Bellevue, WA 98007

Publisher's Cataloging in Publication
(prepared by Quality Books Inc.)

Oberlin, Salley, 1948–
  A Quick Course in Windows, version 3 / Salley Oberlin, Patrick Kervran. —
  p. cm
  Includes index
  ISBN 1-879399-00-8
  1. Microsoft Windows (Computer programs) I. Kervran, Patrick, 1961– II. Title.

QA76.76.W56   005.4'3
                          QBI90-164
                              90-63893
                              CIP

Printed and bound in the United States of America

1 2 3 4 5 6 7 8 9 O L O L 3 2 1 0

Distributed to bookstores by Publishers Group West, (800) 365-3453

Contents

Introduction

For several years now, we've been answering questions from friends, acquaintances, and even strangers about computers and software. Each time we walk a bewildered and sometimes desperate person through a procedure, we wonder why the people who come to us don't use the product documentation or read computer books. Linda is a store manager; Peter runs a sports club; Norma and Ted are school teachers; Barbara works in a law firm; John is a quality-control specialist. They are all educated and astute; they are all used to planning their time, setting goals, and making decisions. What do they have in common that makes it easier for them to call us with their questions rather than rifle through the materials that came with their software?

The answer is that they are all very busy.

They have more important things to do than wade through page after page of documentation or digest a 400-page computer book. They want fast answers and straightforward, easy-to-follow instructions on how to complete the task at hand. They aren't interested in a lot of background information or in learning two approaches to the same task—they just want to get the job done.

If you're a busy professional who wants to know how to integrate Microsoft Windows into your work life, we think you'll find that *A Quick Course in Windows* is just what you've been looking for. In this book, we cover loading Windows, organizing files in a logical fashion for easy retrieval, switching among Windows and non-Windows applications, and sharing information. We show you how to perform everyday tasks and create real-life documents with

Windows' wide range of accessories. We deliberately focus on what you might want to do with Windows, not on what Windows does.

Because not everyone learns in the same way, all Quick Course books accommodate two learning styles. For the person who simply wants to perform the task at hand, the top two-thirds of the page offers no-nonsense, to-the-point guidance. For the person who prefers to understand the whys and wherefores of a program, the bottom third of the page offers additional information about program concepts, shortcuts, jargon, pitfalls, and so on. The books have a special binding that allows them to lay flat on your desk, so you can read them easily while you work at your computer.

There's a well-known saying in the computer industry that 80 percent of the people who buy best-selling software products use only 20 percent of the products' features. What we offer is streamlined instruction for the new user. Because Windows makes *using* the computer quick and easy, we think *learning* Windows should be quick and easy. It is not our intention to describe every command and feature of the program—the manual does that. Instead, we cover only what you need to know to begin using Windows effectively. You can read this book in less than a day and work through the examples in just a few hours. Our goal is to help you integrate Windows into your daily work life with as little fuss as possible.

Enough said. It's time to get back to the computer and put Windows to work.

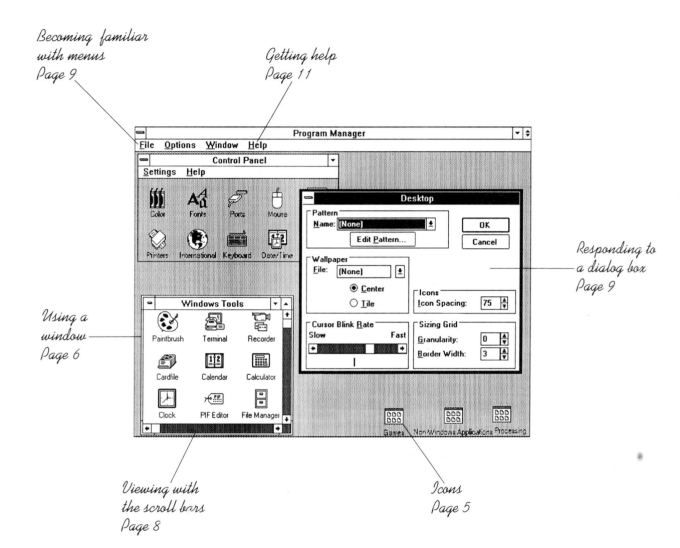

*Becoming familiar
with menus
Page 9*

*Getting help
Page 11*

*Responding to
a dialog box
Page 9*

*Using a
window
Page 6*

*Viewing with
the scroll bars
Page 8*

*Icons
Page 5*

1

What's the Big Deal about Windows?

Sometimes it seems that everywhere you go someone is talking about Microsoft Windows. People who formerly have shown little interest in computers are now touting the convenience of Microsoft's new graphical environment. Computer magazines are awash with Windows articles, and venerable newspapers like the *Wall Street Journal* devote whole columns to analyses of the impact of Windows on the software industry.

Why all the fuss? What makes Windows so special? In this chapter we discuss Windows' main claims to fame. We also describe some of Windows' features that make using your computer easier and more intuitive than ever before, which in turn helps you to be more productive. If you are a recent convert from the Apple Macintosh, or if you are otherwise familiar with the features of graphical interfaces, you may only want to skim this chapter.

A New Way to Communicate

Windows provides an environment, called a *graphical user interface*, that allows you to communicate visually with your computer. With Windows, you no longer have to remember obscure commands and type them at a DOS prompt to make the program work. You simply click a picture called an *icon* or select a command from a list called a *menu* to tell Windows what you want it to do.

Windows applications

The following are some of the programs designed for use with Windows 3.0. New products are constantly being announced.

Accuscan
Adobe Illustrator—
    Windows Version
Adobe Streamline
Adobe TypeManager
Aldus PageMaker
Ami Professional

Ami Word Processing
BatchWorks
BeckenTools for Windows
Bitstream FaceLift
Bookkeeping By Design
CA-Cricket Graph
Calculus
Corel Draw!
Crosstalk for Windows
Designer
Distinct Back-Up
DoDot
Dr. Process
Drafix CAD

Dragnet
Fast!
File Saver
FormBase
Grammatik for Windows
ESA Power Programs
Form Publisher
hDC FirstApps
hDC Windows Express
IBM Current
if:X Personal Tax Analyst
if:X Business Expense
    Reports
Intermission

It is important to understand that Windows is not an operating system like DOS. (The operating system's job is to handle communications between the program you are running and the hardware and software that are actually doing the work.) Windows is just like any other program; you cannot run Windows without DOS. Windows' job resembles that of a translator. You use the Windows environment to give simple visual instructions that Windows then translates into a more complex language that DOS and the computer can understand.

Graphical user interfaces (GUIs) are not new. The Apple Macintosh, which, because of its interface, took the computing world by storm when it was released in 1984, was just one of a series of systems that have used a visual "language" for people/computer communication. However, Windows is the first graphical environment for the huge IBM PC family to gain support in the software industry.

A Common Look

Software-industry support is fundamental to the Windows revolution. In addition to making it easier for you to perform DOS operations, the Windows environment also makes it easier for you to learn and use any application program that has been developed to run under Windows, because the applications all share a common look.

IRMA WorkStation for Windows	MoreFonts	Superbase 2
KnowledgePro Windows	ObjectScript	SuperPrint
Language Master	PreFORM PRO	Tempo for Windows
LanMagic	Publisher's Paintbrush	The Desktop Set
Legacy	Publisher's Powerpak	ToolBook
MacroCalc	PubTech	Ventura Publisher
Micrografx Charisma	R Office+	WinCheck
Micrografx Designer	Read Write Personal	Windows Personal Librarian
Microsoft Excel for Windows	ScrapbookPlus	Windows Spell
Microsoft Powerpoint for Windows	Screen Works	Windows Workstation
Microsoft Project for Windows	Session for Windows	Wingz
Microsoft Word for Windows	SmartApps' Shades	WinSleuth
Milestone's Etc.	SoftType	WinText
	Spinnaker plus	Word Cruncher ◆

Before Windows, PC software developers worked independently to produce application programs, building interfaces that best suited the tasks of their programs. However, Windows developers have been persuaded to produce applications with a common interface and a common way of operating, thus decreasing learning time and enabling people to quickly become as familiar and comfortable with computers as they are with any other piece of equipment in the office.

Easy Transfer of Information

Windows makes it easier than ever before to transfer information from one program to another. Need a logo for your letterhead? You can create one with a paint program, copy it into a temporary storage area called the *Clipboard*, and then paste it into a word-processing document—in three easy steps. Because Windows allows you to run the paint program and the word-processing program simultaneously, moving from one program to the other is a simple matter of clicking a mouse button to switch between windows.

Called *multitasking*, running two or more programs concurrently can save you time by keeping all the information you need at your fingertips, whether it is stored in a report, a spreadsheet, a database, or any other type of file. If you're in the middle of writing a letter and need to look up some figures in a spreadsheet, you no longer have to stop what you are doing, quit the word processor, load the spreadsheet, find the figures, and then start your word processor again. You can simply flip between windows to get the information you need—in only a couple easy steps.

The Visual Language of Windows

Some of the terms you'll run into when using Windows may be new to you. Before we get started with the program, let's make sure we are all speaking the same language.

Icons

An icon is simply a symbol. With Windows, icons are used to represent all sorts of items, including applications, documents, windows, commands, and even network servers. To make using Windows as intuitive as possible, icons are usually easy to associate with the item they represent. For example, the icon for Terminal, the Windows telecommunication program, is a telephone sitting on a modem. In case the symbol is not instantly recognizable, each icon has a name. When you select an icon to do something with it, the area behind its name changes color.

Pointer

The pointer is a symbol that represents on the screen the movements you make with your mouse when you work. The pointer is usually an arrow, but it can take the form of a hand (when using Help), an I-beam, a text cursor (in a word processor), or an hourglass (when Windows is processing information). In a paint program such as Windows Paintbrush, the pointer changes shape with each tool you use; for example, it might take the shape of a pencil or a paintbrush.

Mouse

Some veteran PC users are convinced that Windows is part of a grand plot to make them use a mouse, and there is no question that working with Windows is a lot easier with one.

Windows icons vs. Mac icons

If you are converting to Windows from the Macintosh, your mouse and window-handling skills will come in handy in the Windows environment. But toss out any preconceived ideas about icons! Icons in the Windows environment bear no real relation to the files they represent. For example, deleting a program icon in Program Manager doesn't delete the program; it simply deletes the icon! Similarly, duplicating an icon doesn't duplicate the document or program it represents; it simply makes a copy of the icon. ♦

When you need advice

The telephone number for Microsoft Product Support Services is (206) 454-2030. A message may tell you to call an 800 number if you need sales and services. For questions about operating Windows, stay on the line and push the specified button to route your call to a Windows expert. ♦

Once you learn how to use a mouse proficiently, you'll use it as often as you use the keyboard. Using the mouse to pull down menus, select commands, scroll through windows, and so forth is much easier than performing the same operations with the keyboard. Of course, you'll still use the keyboard to type text.

Windows

Windows are rectangular portions of the screen in which you view a group of icons that represent programs or other windows, or the contents of a file. Except when you are using a non-Windows application, everything you see in Windows is in a window.

All windows have a title bar, a frame, and a menu bar. A window may also have buttons and scroll bars.

Control menu Title bar

Menu bar Buttons

Scroll bar

Pointing	Clicking	Double-clicking
Moving the mouse around on your desktop moves the pointer on your screen. To point to an item, simply move the mouse so that the pointer rests over that item. ♦	You click the mouse button to activate icons and windows, to resize windows, and to open menus. You also click options to select them. Clicking is simply a matter of pressing and releasing the left mouse button once. You also click to activate an insertion point in text so that you can make changes. This is called *clicking an insertion point.* ♦	You double-click to start programs and open windows. Double-clicking works the same as clicking, except that you *quickly* click the mouse button twice. ♦

Title bar   At the top of every window is a title bar, which describes the function of the window or shows the name of the program or document displayed in it. When a window is active, its title bar is dark in color indicating that the next action you perform will affect that window. When a window is not active, its title bar is light in color.

Window frame   All windows have frames, and most frames can stretch and shrink to make their windows bigger or smaller. As you move the pointer over different parts of resizable frames, the pointer turns into a double-headed arrow, indicating the directions in which you can drag the frame. Drag the sides of the frame to the left and right, drag the top and bottom of the frame up and down, and drag the corners up and down diagonally.

Menu bar   Across the top of every window is a menu bar, which shows the menus available for use with the items displayed in that particular window. A menu is a list of commands that carry out related tasks.

Every menu bar has at least one menu, the Control menu. The Control menu lists commands that take the place of some mouse actions, such as moving and resizing windows. Other commands allow you to close a window, switch between open document windows, and switch to other open applications. The Control menu is not only available in each window but it also appears in some dialog boxes (discussed shortly).

Dragging

Dragging repositions an icon or a window on the screen and resizes windows. Start by pointing at the item you want to drag, and click. Then hold down the mouse button while moving the mouse. A "ghost" image of the icon or window follows the pointer. Release the button when the image is where you want it. The icon or window then moves to the new position. ♦

Selecting characters

You identify text you want to cut, copy, or format by selecting it. Selecting text characters is probably the most difficult thing you'll have to do with your mouse. Click to the left of the first character you want to select, drag the mouse to the right of the last character, and then release the mouse button. You can also drag upward or downward to select entire lines at once. The selected text becomes dark in color. You can then cut, copy, or format the text. ♦

Buttons   The buttons on windows are usually shaped like arrows. For example, many windows have one or two arrows in their top-right corner, which enable you to resize the window quickly. Clicking the Minimize button—the down arrow—shrinks the window down to an icon. Minimizing a window is a quick way of tucking the window out of the way without quitting the program or file that is displayed in the window. Clicking the Maximize button—the up arrow—expands the window to the size of the full screen. Maximizing a window gives you a larger working space when you are running an application, but obscures any other windows. The Restore button (a double-headed arrow) appears only on maximized windows in place of the Maximize button to allow you to quickly return the maximized window to its previous size.

Scroll bars   Even when maximized, windows are often not big enough to display all of their contents, particularly if the file you have loaded is a long document or a large spreadsheet. If more information appears in a window than can fit, scroll bars appear to help you view invisible parts of the screen. You use scroll bars to bring hidden contents into view. Windows can have scroll bars on their bottom and right sides, depending on how much of the window is out of view. You use the right scroll bar to move the contents up and down in the window and the bottom scroll bar to move the contents from side to side.

Learning to use the scroll bars is crucial to using Windows. You can use several different scrolling methods. Clicking the arrows at the ends of the scroll bars moves the contents a line or a column at a time, whereas clicking on either side of the boxes in the scroll bars moves them a windowful at a time. You can also drag the scroll boxes to a new position in the scroll bar. Their position roughly indicates the position of the window in relation to its contents. For example, when the scroll box is in the middle of the scroll bar, the window is positioned roughly halfway through its contents.

Desktop

The Windows background screen, on which all windows and icons appear, is known as the *desktop*. This well-worn metaphor is designed to make using the tools available with

Windows no more intimidating than using the familiar tools found on a typical desk in a typical office.

One Windows program, Program Manager, always appears on the desktop, either as an icon or a window. If you want to jazz up your desktop, you can use Program Manager's Control Panel to change the color and pattern of the background. You can even use a graphic as desktop "wallpaper." But be forewarned: Icons don't show up very well against complex illustrations.

Menus and Commands

To carry out most tasks, you need to choose commands from menus. Click the name of the menu you want in the menu bar, and the menu drops down, displaying a list of commands. To choose a command, click the command name.

Some command names are displayed in "gray" letters, indicating that you can't choose those commands at this time. For example, the Maximize command appears in gray when the window is already maximized.

Some command names are followed by an ellipsis (...), indicating that you must supply more information in a special kind of window called a *dialog box* before the command can be carried out.

As part of the effort to give all Windows applications a common look, menus with similar functions and commands that carry out similar tasks often have the same names in different applications. The Control menu, File menu, Window menu, and Help menu are examples of common menus. In all likelihood, the File menu will be the menu you use most often. This menu usually contains commands such as New (for creating new windows or documents), Open (for opening windows or documents), Save (for saving the current document), and Exit or Close (to leave the current program, or to leave Windows).

Dialog Boxes

Dialog boxes are Windows' way of communicating with you, either when it needs to give you a message or warning or when you need to give information or select from several different options in order for a particular command to be

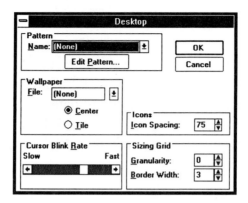

carried out. You usually give information by typing in a text box. Options may appear in scrolling lists, in drop-down lists, with checkmark buttons, or with radio buttons. Other dialog-box buttons, such as Cancel and OK, allow you to confirm your selections or give other instructions.

Scrolling lists   When more options are available than can fit in the dialog box, they are displayed on a scrolling list. You scroll the list in the same way you scroll a window: Simply click the arrows at either end of the scroll bar. Make a selection by clicking one of the options to highlight it.

Drop-down lists   Initially, a drop-down list box appears in the dialog box as a rectangle containing a highlighted option. To the right of the box is a down-pointing arrow, which indicates that other options are available if the highlighted one doesn't meet your needs. Clicking the arrow drops down a list of the other options, from which you can make a selection by clicking. Drop-down list boxes that are too long to fit in the dialog box have scroll bars, which you use just like those in scrolling list boxes.

Checkmark buttons   Checkmark buttons are small square boxes. When you click an empty checkmark button to select the associated option, an *X* appears in the button to indicate that the option is active, or turned on. Clicking the button again removes the *X* to indicate that the option is inactive, or turned off. Checkmark buttons operate independently of one another, so from a group of checkmark buttons you can select none, one, or all the options, as required for the task at hand.

Radio buttons   Radio buttons are round and they always appear in a group of mutually exclusive options. When you click a radio button, a black bullet appears in the button to indicate that the option is active. Because only one of the group of buttons can be active at a time, the bullet disappears from the button of the previously active option.

Text boxes   You enter variable information, such as a file name, in a dialog box by typing it in a text box. If text is already displayed in the text box and you want to replace the text, you can select the text box by clicking it and then simply overtype the old text with the new.

Other buttons   Clicking OK closes the dialog box and carries out the command according to the settings. Clicking Cancel closes the dialog box and also cancels the command.

Some dialog boxes have other buttons that refine the original command or open yet another dialog box with more options. You select options from the second dialog box in the same way as the first. Clicking OK or Cancel closes the second box and returns you to the first.

Warning messages   Windows applications display messages and warnings in dialog boxes when a command can't be carried out or when there is a chance you might regret having issued the command—for example, when deleting files. Clicking Cancel or No cancels the command and closes the warning dialog box, whereas clicking OK or Yes acknowledges the message and continues the command.

Getting Help

Using Windows is fairly intuitive, and this book will help you find your way around so that, most of the time, you will know exactly what to do and how. However, for those times when you stumble over a particular operation, Windows provides an excellent, powerful, Help feature. Think of the Help feature as an encyclopedia-sized book that you can page through for help.

A full program in its own right, Help can be accessed by pressing the F1 key or by choosing a topic from the Help menu that appears in most Windows applications. Usually, the Help menu has an Index command that gives you a broad view of the Help topics available for that application. Other commands, such as Keyboard, Commands, Procedures, and Using Help, narrow down the Help topics.

When you press F1 or choose a Help topic, the Help program is loaded into its own resizable, scrolling window, with menus from which you can choose commands. For example, you can use the Menu command to print the displayed Help-file page, annotate a topic with your own comments, or insert a bookmark so that you can readily return to an important bit of information.

Buttons at the top of the Help window take you to the Help index and then back to the Help screen, allow you to browse forward and backward through the Help file a page at a time, and let you search for a particular topic.

A shaded line appears when more information is available about a specific topic elsewhere in the Help file. When you point to the line, the pointer changes to a hand icon, indicating that if you click the line, you will be taken directly to the additional information.

The About command, which is the last command on many Help menus, can also provide some vital information about the program you are running. In addition to showing you the version number of the program, this command may also tell you what mode you are running in and how much free memory you have available, as well as esoteric tidbits like whether or not your machine has a math coprocessor.

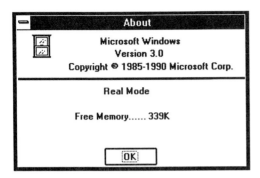

With this background information under your belt, you are ready to get started with the Windows program. If you have not yet installed Windows on your computer, turn to Appendix A. While using the Windows Setup program, you will have a chance to apply your knowledge about windows, dialog boxes, and a host of other features. If your computer is all set to start running Windows, head on to Chapter 2, where we get down to work with the program.

Windows newsletters

ACKnowledge, The Windows Letter
144 Talmadge Road
Mendham, NJ 07945
(201) 543-6033

For Windows Only
PJM Communications
PO Box 6172
Burbank, CA 91510
(818) 563-4285

Inside Microsoft Windows
The Cobb Group, Inc.
9420 Bunsen Parkway, Suite 300
Louisville, KY 40220
(800) 223-8720

OS/2 and Windows Magazine
The Silicon Beach Operation
1101B Eugenia Place
Carpinteria, CA 93013
(805) 566-1282

View, The WPMA Newsletter
Windows & Presentation Manager Association

1521 N. Glenville
Richardson, TX 75085
(214) 234-8857

Windows Watcher
CompuTh!nk, Incorporated
3731 130th Ave. NE
Bellevue, WA 98005
(206) 881-7354

WUGNET Journal
WUGNET Publications, Inc.
1295 N. Providence Road
Media, PA 19063
(215) 565-1861 ♦

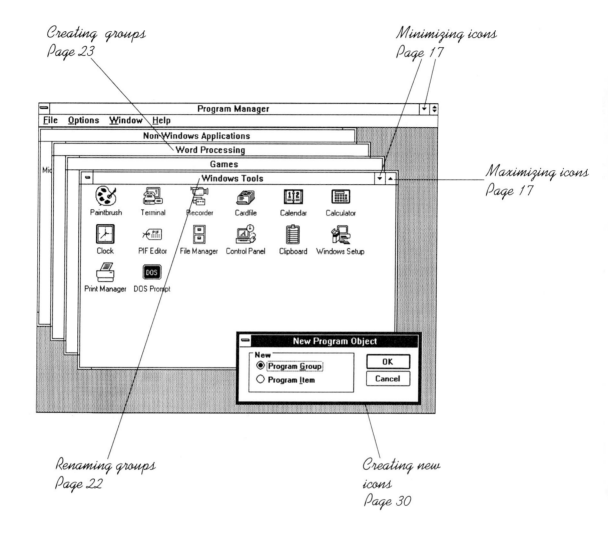

Creating groups
Page 23

Minimizing icons
Page 17

Maximizing icons
Page 17

Renaming groups
Page 22

Creating new
icons
Page 30

Program Manager

File   Options   Window   Help

Non-Windows Applications

Word Processing

Games

Windows Tools

Paintbrush   Terminal   Recorder   Cardfile   Calendar   Calculator

Clock   PIF Editor   File Manager   Control Panel   Clipboard   Windows Setup

Print Manager   DOS Prompt

New Program Object

New
● Program Group
○ Program Item

OK
Cancel

2

Windows Working Environment

C hapter 1 explained some of the concepts behind Windows. Now you're ready to integrate this new program into your everyday work. First, if you haven't already done so, load Windows by simply typing *win* at the C> prompt and pressing Enter. The first time you run Windows, your screen looks like this:

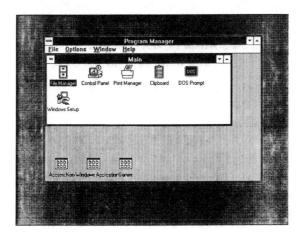

Windows has two distinct components that help you get organized and thereby contribute to your productivity: Program Manager and File Manager. Program Manager helps you organize your work into logical, manageable groups and gives you the tools to create and manipulate files. File Manager helps you clean up your hard disk so that your programs and documents are stored in an efficient, easily

Windows modes

Windows can run in one of three modes: Real, Standard, and 386 Enhanced. The mode depends primarily on your processor chip and memory configuration. When you start Windows by typing *win* at the C> prompt, the program runs in the most powerful mode possible. To run in a less powerful mode, type the commands given in the mode descriptions. ♦

Real mode

Type *win /r* to run in Real mode. Real mode is used by IBM PCs and XTs (with Intel 8086 and 8088 chips). It can access only 640 KB of memory, the standard DOS limitation, even if more memory is available. Because Windows itself uses about 75 KB of memory, available memory is less than 640 KB. Real mode allows limited multitasking among Windows

applications, and it allows you to run non-Windows applications without multitasking. Because of memory restrictions, switching between programs can require moving data from RAM to disk and back again, which slows down operation considerably. You may have to run Windows in Real mode to use applications created for Windows versions earlier than 3.0. ♦

accessible manner. We cover File Manager in Chapter 3. In this chapter, we introduce you to Program Manager.

Program Manager is loaded automatically when you start Windows. It runs throughout your Windows work session. Your computer is now displaying the Program Manager screen. When Windows was installed on your computer, the Windows Setup program sorted the Windows component programs into groups, such as the Accessories group, the Games group, and the Main group. If your hard disk contains Windows applications, such as Microsoft Word for Windows, or non-Windows applications, such as Lotus 1-2-3 Release 2.2, Windows also created groups for those applications. The window titled *Main* that you now see in the middle of the screen represents the Main group, a collection of tools that come with Windows. The icons at the bottom of the Program Manager screen also represent groups. But because Windows assumes you don't need these groups when you first load the program, instead of opening windows for all of them, Windows has "minimized" the groups into small icons to reduce screen clutter.

Minimizing and Maximizing Icons

Windows allows you to minimize (shrink) windows into icons and maximize (expand) icons into windows as you need to. Try the following procedure.

Standard mode

Type *win /s* to run in Standard mode. Standard mode is used by IBM PC ATs and PS/2s (with Intel 80286 and 80386 chips) with at least 1 MB of memory. This mode takes advantage of all available system memory up to 16 MB, but non-Windows applications are still limited to 640 KB. Multitasking is possible among Windows applications, but not between non-Windows and Windows applications. As in Real mode, inactive programs in Standard mode may go to disk when memory is overloaded. ◆

386 Enhanced mode

Type *win /3* to run in 386 Enhanced mode. 386 Enhanced mode is used by computers with the Intel 80386 chip and at least 2 MB of memory. It allows true multitasking, even among non-Windows applications. It also allows non-Windows applications to run in windows with Control menus so that you can copy and paste data between applications. ◆

1. Using the mouse, click the Minimize button (the down arrow) in the top-right corner of the Main window. The window shrinks into an icon and moves to the bottom of the Program Manager screen. Notice that the name *Main* appears beneath the icon.

2. Give yourself some working room by fully expanding the Program Manager window. Click the Maximize button (the up arrow) in the top-right corner of the Program Manager window. The window expands to fill the screen.

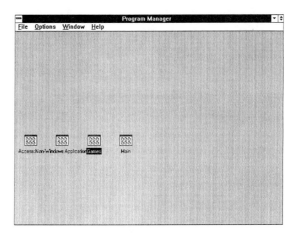

3. To expand the Main icon back to the Main window, double-click the Main icon.

Arranging Windows

After opening several windows, you may find your screen a jumble of obscured and partially visible windows. Two commands on the Window menu, Tile and Cascade, can help you clean up your act.

1. Open the Accessories window by double-clicking its icon at the bottom of the screen. This window may now partially obscure the Main window, so you need to rearrange the windows. You could resize and reposition the windows using the mouse, but a faster way is to use either the Cascade or the Tile command.

2. Choose the Cascade command from the Window menu. The windows arrange themselves in a neat

stack, with the title bar and left edge of the bottom (or obscured) window showing.

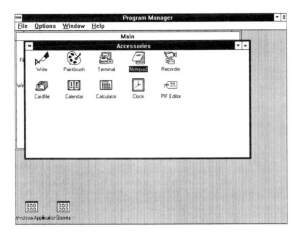

Notice that the title bar of the Accessories window is dark in color, whereas the title bar of the Main window is light in color. The dark title bar indicates that the window is active, meaning that it is the window that will be affected by your next action.

Although the Cascade command neatly arranges the windows, you may prefer to position them so that you can see as much of both of them as possible. For this purpose, you can use the Tile command, which arranges all open windows on the screen like tiles on a kitchen floor. Try this:

1. Choose Tile from the Window menu. The windows reposition themselves so that they each take up about

---

Disappearing windows

Window "logic" can be baffling to first time users. Common problems are "lost" and obscured windows. Think of your open windows as playing cards in a deck. The topmost window is completely visible, but successive windows get buried. They are still there; they are just not visible. ♦

Tile vs. Cascade

Although Tile may seem like the obvious choice to organize your workspace, it can create some confusion. Window groups with many icons will shrink down to make room for other windows and may not have room to display all of their icons. Use the Cascade command if you are arranging more than four or five windows. ♦

Directories vs. groups

Organizing your programs into groups in Program Manager does not affect the way your directories and files are stored. You use groups to visually arrange program icons for ease of use under Program Manager. However, moving a program icon from one group to another does not actually move the program on your hard disk. ♦

half of the screen, with space left at the bottom for the other group icons.

Reorganizing Groups

One of the great things about Windows is that it is highly customizable. In Program Manager, you can reorganize, delete, copy, and even create elements. For example, when you start working with Windows, you may find yourself wondering why Windows organized its component programs the way it did. In particular, you may find that the separation of certain programs into Main and Accessories groups is confusing and even illogical. Putting them all into one group is as easy as dragging their icons from one window to another. Try the following:

1. Activate the Main window by clicking anywhere within it.
2. Click the File Manager icon in the Main window. The name under the icon becomes dark in color, indicating that it is active.
3. Hold down the mouse button and drag the icon into the Accessories window. Release the mouse button. As you drag the icon, its colors may change, and the name under the icon disappears. This is perfectly normal. And don't worry about arranging the icons neatly in the Accessories window. You'll rearrange them later.

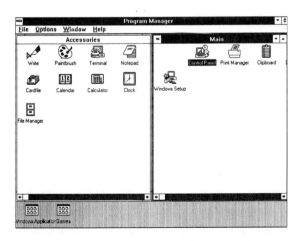

4. Repeat the previous step for the remaining icons in the Main window, until you have moved all the icons to the Accessories window. If the Main window has scroll bars, some of the icons are not visible, and you'll need to use the scroll arrow in the bottom-right corner to display them. When you have scrolled all the icons into view, the scroll bars disappear.

Now you've got all the programs that came with Windows (except for the games) in one group.

Deleting Obsolete Groups

If reorganizing the programs and documents in your groups results in a group that no longer contains any icons, you can delete the group so that it does not get in your way. (If it turns out later that you need the group, you can always create a new one, as discussed on page 23.)

Now that the Main group is empty, follow these steps to delete it:

1. Check to be sure that the Main window is active (that its title bar is dark in color), and then choose the Delete command from the File menu. A warning message asks whether you want to delete the Main group.

2. Click Yes. The Main window disappears from the screen, and the Accessories window becomes active.

Arranging Icons

Messy windows are hard to work with, and the more icons you add to a group, the messier the group's window can become. You'll probably want to straighten up the icons in the Accessories window to make them easier to locate. You could do this by carefully positioning each icon with the mouse, but there is an easier way:

1. With the Accessories window active, choose Arrange Icons from the Window menu. Windows aligns the icons so that they fit in the Accessories window in perfect rows and columns.

Windows can also automatically rearrange icons for you each time you open a window or change window sizes.

1. Click the Options menu. If you don't see a checkmark in front of the Auto Arrange command, choose Auto Arrange to make it active.

Renaming Groups

The current name of this group, Accessories, no longer fits the collection of programs in the group, so let's change the name to something more appropriate. Here's how:

1. Shrink the Accessories window to an icon by clicking the Minimize button in the top-right corner of the Accessories window.
2. Make the Accessories icon active by clicking it once. A menu pops up above the icon. This is the icon's Control menu, and you can ignore it for now. (We discuss Control menus on page 7.)
3. Choose the Properties command from the File menu. A dialog box appears with the group name highlighted.

4. Type *Windows Tools* as the new name for the group, and then click OK. The new name replaces the old one beneath the group icon at the bottom of the Program Manager screen.

5. Double-click the Windows Tools icon to expand it into a window. The new name for the group appears in the window's title bar.

You can change the name of any icon, even a program icon, to a name of up to 40 characters. However, changing the name of a Windows icon doesn't actually change the name of the document or application it represents. As far as DOS is concerned, the document or application still has its original name of eight or fewer characters. The icon name is merely a device to enable you to more easily manage files within Windows.

Creating New Groups

You may now want to organize other groups in Program Manager to suit your needs. One constructive technique is to create a group for each of your current projects and to include all relevant documents in the group. Double-clicking a project group icon would then automatically open a window that would put everything you need to work on that project at your fingertips.

Minimizing the wrong window

If you minimize the Program Manager window by mistake, all that appears on the screen is the Program Manager icon and any icons for other open programs. You can easily backtrack by double-clicking the icon to maximize the Program Manager icon. Then minimize the correct window. ♦

No groups within groups

Group windows cannot be placed within other group windows. Group windows are strictly one-dimensional and are intended only to organize icons into logical collections. If you try to move a minimized window into another group window, the group icon simply floats above the window. ♦

No lone-wolf icons

Icons must be placed in a group. You can organize them by dragging them to group windows or by dragging them to minimized window icons, but they must be part of a group. If you try to place an icon outside a group window, the icon turns into an international "no" icon (a circle with a diagonal slash through it), indicating that you can't do it. ♦

In the next exercise, you will create a new group to hold word-processing applications, including the Notepad and Write programs that come with Windows and any other writing programs you might have, such as Word for Windows. You will also create two simple documents and store them as document icons with the writing programs. Follow these steps:

1. Choose the New command from the File menu. The New Program Object dialog box appears.
2. Click the Program Group button, and then click OK. The Program Group Properties dialog box appears.

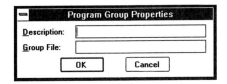

3. In the Description text box, type *Word Processing*, the name for the new group, and click OK. A new, empty group window appears, overlapping the Windows Tools window.
4. Choose the Tile command from the Window menu. The windows reposition themselves on the screen so that they no longer overlap.
5. Click the Write icon, drag the icon into the Word Processing window, and release the mouse button.
6. Click the Notepad icon, drag the icon into the Word Processing window, and release the mouse button.

You can repeat this procedure for any other Windows "text cruncher" applications you own, such as Word for Windows or Ami Professional, whose icons will be stored in the Windows Applications group. You can also use the new Word Processing group to store non-Windows applications such as Word or WordPerfect, whose icons will be stored in the Non-Windows Applications window. Using the same techniques, you could also create a group called *Correspondence* in which to keep business letters, or a group called *Quarterly Projections* for spreadsheets.

Creating Documents

Next, we'll create a simple document in the Word Processing group and watch Windows assign it an appropriate icon. For this purpose, you'll use Notepad, the handy text editor that is shipped with Windows. Notepad is useful for jotting down notes or creating and editing short text documents.

For this exercise, assume that CityRock Gym, a sports club in Emeryville, California, which features indoor rock climbing and weight training, is investigating the cost of purchasing a small public-address system. During a phone conversation, Peter Mayfield, the club's manager, might want to take down information about a potential supplier. Let's follow along with the steps:

1. Double-click the Notepad icon in the Word Processing window. The Notepad application opens with a blank, untitled document displayed. Notice that the Notepad window is not maximized, allowing you to see parts of other windows. In Chapter 4, you'll learn how to activate these windows so that you can switch among open applications and move information from one to another.

2. The blinking insertion point in the top-left corner of the Notepad window indicates that you can begin typing, so type *Allphone, Inc.* (the supplier's name), and press Enter.

Exiting gracefully	Opening the Next window	The Run command
The Exit command can be found on the File menu of all Windows applications. It allows you to quit the current application and return to the previously opened program. If an application doesn't have a File menu, use the Close command on the Control menu. ♦	Another way to activate windows or group window icons in Program Manager is to use the Next command, which is on the Control menu of all group windows. Choosing this command activates the window or window icon that was opened after the currently active window. You can also press Ctrl-Tab to cycle quickly through windows. ♦	The Run command allows you to run Windows or non-Windows programs by typing the program name and clicking OK. If the program is not located in the current directory, type the entire path (see page 44).You can use the Run command to start programs that you use infrequently and for which you don't want to create an icon. ♦

3. Type *4107 Lake Louis Ave, Ste 44*, and press Enter.
4. Type *Emeryville, CA 94608*, and press Enter.
5. Type *(415) 666-2000*, and press Enter.

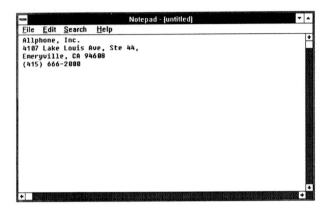

Now save the document:

1. Choose the Save As command from the File menu. The File Save As dialog box appears.

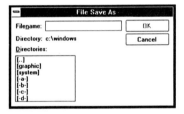

2. In the Filename text box, type *pubadsys* (for *public-address system*), and click OK. Because you haven't specified a directory and file-name extension, the document is saved in the WINDOWS directory and is given the extension TXT, which indicates that the file was created by the Notepad program. When the file is saved, the name of the file, PUBADSYS.TXT appears in the title bar of the window.

3. Choose the Exit command from the File menu. The Notepad window closes, and you return to Program Manager.

Next, you need to specify the icon and the name you want the document to have when it is displayed in the Program Manager window. You can give the document any name that will help you remember what it is.

1. Click the Word Processing window, and choose New from the File menu. The New dialog box appears.
2. Click Program Item, and then click OK. The Program Item Properties dialog box appears.

3. In the Description text box, type *PA System* as the name of this document.
4. Click the Command Line text box, and associate the new icon name with the DOS filename by typing *c:\windows\pubadsys.txt.*
5. Click the Change Icon button, and the Select Icon dialog box appears. The icon that Windows has selected for the document is displayed in the Current Selection area. You can change the icon to something that will remind you what the document is about.
6. Click the View Next button repeatedly to cycle through the available icons. When you find one that is appropriate, click OK.
7. Click OK in the Program Item Properties dialog box to close the box and return to Program Manager.

In the Word Processing window, you can now see the new icon with the name *PA System* below it.

Transferring Information via the Clipboard

Imagine that later in the day you decide to transfer the supplier's name and address from Notepad to the Write program so that you can write a letter inquiring about their public-address systems:

1. Double-click the PA System icon in the Word Processing window. The PUBADSYS.TXT document is loaded into a Notepad window.

2. Select the text in the window by pointing to the left of the first character of the supplier's name, holding down the left mouse button, and dragging down and to the right until all the information is highlighted.

3. Choose Copy from the Edit menu.

4. Choose Exit from the File menu.

Although you have closed the Notepad window, the copied text still exists on the Clipboard, a temporary storage place for cut or copied data. Let's sidetrack here for a moment to make sure the text is on the Clipboard:

1. Double-click the Clipboard icon in the Windows Tools window. The Clipboard opens, revealing the text you have copied.

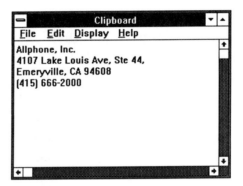

The Clipboard tool

The Clipboard is an area of memory where cut or copied data is stored temporarily, but it is also a Windows tool that allows you to view that data. You cannot manipulate it, even though Clipboard has an Edit menu. The only actions you can take, besides simple viewing, are to save the Clipboard contents as a file or to clear the contents. ♦

Saving Clipboard contents

If you cannot immediately paste cut or copied information, you can save the contents of the Clipboard as a file. Double-click the Clipboard icon to open its window, and choose Save As from the File menu. Give the file any eight-character name, using the CLP extension so that Clipboard recognizes the file. ♦

Freeing memory

If you are running low on memory, clearing the contents of the Clipboard storage area may free some up. Double-click the Clipboard icon to open its window, and choose Delete from the Edit menu. ♦

2. Close the Clipboard by choosing the Exit command from the File menu. Now paste the copied text into a Write document.

3. Double-click the Write icon in the Word Processing window. Windows loads the program, which displays a blank document window.

4. Choose Paste from the Edit menu. The text you copied from the Notepad document now appears in the Write window.

5. Complete the letter of inquiry with the date, a brief description of the system you need, and a request for information. Then save the document.

6. Choose Save As from the File menu. The File Save As dialog box appears so that you can give the Write file a name.

7. Type *pas20490*, which stands for *public address system inquiry on February 4, 1990*. Click OK. The name of the file, PAS20490.WRI appears in the Write window's title bar. (Write gives all files it creates a .WRI extension unless you tell it otherwise.)

8. Close the window and quit the Write program by choosing Exit from the File menu.

Another Way to Assign Icons

To create an icon for the letter, you can repeat the steps you went through to create an icon for the PUBADSYS.TXT document, but there is another way to do it. You may have noticed that when you chose an icon for the PUBADSYS.TXT document, you were limited to a few icons. Wouldn't it be helpful if you could assign the icon for the parent program to the document to make it easier to remember which application created it? Here's how to do it:

1. Holding down the Ctrl key, click the Write icon, and drag it to another place within the Word Processing window. A copy of the Write icon appears.

2. With the Write icon active, select the Properties command from the File menu. The Program Items Properties dialog box appears.

3. In the Description text box, type *PA System Letter*.

4. Click the Command Line text box, which highlights WRITE.EXE. Type *c:\windows\pas20490.wri*, and then click OK.

You return to the Word Processing window, where you'll notice that the name of the Write icon is now PA System Letter. Double-clicking this icon will open the Write program and load the PAS20490.WRI document. Do this now:

1. Double-click the PA System Letter document icon. The PAS20490.WRI document opens in a Write window.

2. Choose Exit from the Write program's File menu.

Creating Icons for New Applications

You can run Windows Setup to include new applications in your groups, but Setup recognizes only certain programs and ignores others. If you have a new application that you want to create an icon for in Program Manager, here is a sure-fire, quick way to do it:

1. Activate the group window that you want to add the application to, and choose New from the File menu.

2. Click the Program Item radio button, and click OK.

3. In the dialog box that appears, type a name for the program in the Description text box and the program's path (see page 44 for more information) in the Command Line text box. You can then select an icon for the program by clicking the Change Icon button. Click View Next to cycle through available icons.

4. When you are finished, click OK in both dialog boxes.

The new program icon appears in the active group. Simply double-click this icon to start the program.

Cleaning Up and Exiting

After you have finished these exercises, your Program Manager window may be a bit of a mess, with various icons and windows strewn about. Now is a good time to get organized before moving on to the next chapter.

1. Open all the remaining windows by double-clicking the group icons at the bottom of the screen. You should have at least one group that you haven't yet inspected: the Games group, which includes the Windows games Reversi and Solitaire. You may also have a group for Windows applications and another for non-Windows applications, depending on what programs you had on your computer when the Setup program was run.

2. Choose Cascade from the Window menu. Your windows reposition themselves in a neat stack.

After you've positioned your windows to your liking, you will want to save the arrangement. The only way to do this is to quit Windows.

1. Choose Exit Windows from the Program Manager File menu. The Exit Windows dialog box appears, warning you that you are about to end your Windows session. By default, the Save Changes option is selected, meaning that the arrangement of your group windows and icons will be saved for your next Windows session.

2. Click OK to save your window and icon arrangement and exit Windows.

That's all there is to it. You may feel a bit overwhelmed because we covered a lot in this chapter, but after you perform these tasks once or twice, they'll seem like old hat.

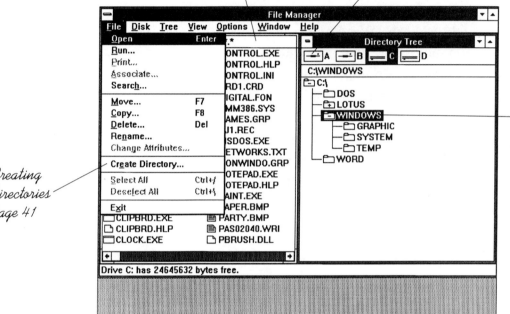

Viewing folders
Page 36

Copying to a
floppy disk
Page 47

Creating
directories
Page 41

Displaying
directories
Page 35

3

Organizing Your Files

For some people, keeping computer files organized has always been a difficult chore. They'll load a program, start a new document, save it with a name such as JOHN.LET or EXPENSES.DAT, and think they'll be able to retrieve the document without much trouble if they ever need it again. Because these people are busy, they often don't take the time to work out a directory- and file-naming system, and they may end up searching directory after directory for the particular file they need. Is it JOHN.LET? Or JSMITH.LET? Or JS1-14.LET? And is it stored in the CORRESP directory, the PROJECTS directory, or the ACCT-REC directory?

With Windows, you no longer have to trust your memory to organize and retrieve documents efficiently. The Windows File Manager program is a powerful hard-disk organizational aid that displays your directories as "tree" diagrams and offers a wide selection of file management tools. If you are working on a network, File Manager may display not only your own drives but all the network drives that are available to you.

Opening File Manager

File Manager

To open File Manager, simply double-click the File Manager icon in Program Manager. (The icon looks like a file cabinet.) If you followed along with the exercises in the last chapter, the icon is in the Windows Tools group. Otherwise, the icon is in the Main group.

When you open File Manager, its window looks something like this:

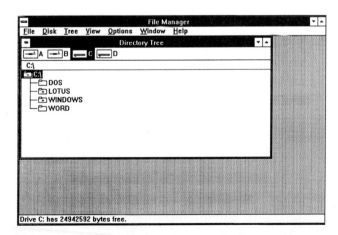

Your File Manager window reflects your hard disk setup and whether you are working on a network. As you can see, a window labeled *Directory Tree* appears within the File Manager window. Below the title bar of the Directory Tree window are icons representing your floppy disk drives, your hard drives (or hard drive partitions), and, if you are connected to a network, the network drives available to you. A letter to the right of each drive icon identifies the drive, and network drive icons are further identified by the letters *NET*.

When first opened, File Manager highlights the C: drive icon and displays a visual diagram in the Directory Tree window of the drive's structure. The directories that "branch" off from the main, or root, directory on your C: drive are represented by folder icons. At the bottom of the File Manager window, a message tells you how much free space you have on the current drive.

Your Directory Tree window contains, at a minimum, icons for a floppy drive (A:) and a single hard drive (C:). The display for your C: drive includes, at a minimum, folders for a DOS directory (which stores operating system files) and a WINDOWS directory.

Displaying Directories

You can expand and contract directories, displaying only the highest directory levels or zooming in for a closer look at subdirectories and files. A plus symbol on a directory folder

---

File Manager icons

File Manager identifies subdirectories, programs, and data files with different icons. Subdirectories have a folder icon; executable files (those with PIF, EXE, BAT, and COM extensions) have rectangular icons with a thin bar across the top; and document files (those that you have created with a specific program) have square icons with thin rules across them. ♦

Quick icons

To quickly create an icon in Program Manager for a document or a program, drag the file icon from the File Manager window into the Program Manager window. An appropriate Program Manager icon, complete with the name of the file, is created. Both the Program Manager window and the File Manager window must be visible for this procedure to work. ♦

The Print command

The Print command on the File menu allows you to print unformatted text files without first opening them. Select the file and choose Print, and File Manager will send the file to Print Manager, or directly to the printer. Use the document's parent application to print anything other than unformatted text. ♦

icon indicates that subdirectories "branch" from that directory and that you can view the subdirectories by clicking the directory folder icon. A minus symbol on a directory folder indicates that you can hide its subdirectories.

In the previous illustration, you may have noticed a minus symbol on the C: folder in the top-left corner of the Directory Tree window and the plus symbol on the WINDOWS folder. Let's take a moment to experiment with hiding and displaying folders:

1. Click the C: folder once. (Be sure to click the folder icon, not the folder name.) The folders representing directories that branch from the root directory disappear (collapse) and the minus symbol on the C: folder icon becomes a plus symbol.

2. Click the C: folder again. The folders reappear (expand) and the plus symbol changes back to a minus symbol.

3. Click the WINDOWS folder once. The WINDOWS directory has, at a minimum, a SYSTEM subdirectory and often you will also have a TEMP subdirectory.

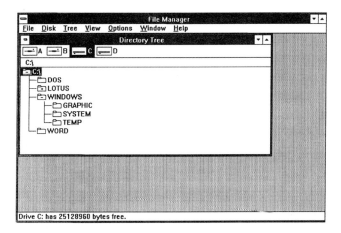

4. Click the WINDOWS folder again to return to the original screen.

Viewing Folders

Expanding and collapsing folders in the Directory Tree window is a quick way to navigate through directories, but you can also open the folders and list the files stored in the subdirectories they represent. Try the following:

1. Double-click the WINDOWS folder. File Manager first expands the folder icon and displays folders for the subdirectories within the WINDOWS directory. Then a directory window appears, listing all the subdirectories and files that are stored in the WINDOWS directory.

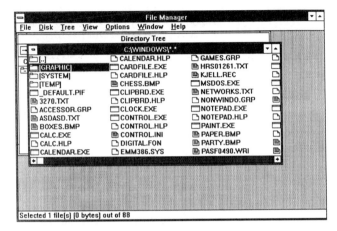

2. Double-click the SYSTEM folder near the top of the window. File Manager opens a new directory window listing the contents of the SYSTEM folder. All the folders within the WINDOWS folder can be opened to display a directory window.

3. Double-click the [..] icon at the top of the SYSTEM directory window. The two dots represent the next highest level in the directory structure—in this case, the WINDOWS directory. The SYSTEM window closes and you return to the WINDOWS directory window.

The SYSTEM directory	**The TEMP directory**	**[..] folder**
The SYSTEM directory contains the files necessary to run Windows. A complex environment like Windows is the sum of many parts. The SYSTEM directory houses programs used to print, draw the screen, recognize mouse actions, produce sound, interpret keyboard input, as well as many other less obvious functions. ♦	Windows creates a TEMP directory as a storage place for the temporary files it generates while you are working with some of its programs. These files all have a TMP extension. If you are running out of room on your hard drive, the TEMP directory is a good place to look for files to delete. You can remove any TMP files with dates other than the current date. ♦	Double-clicking this icon, which appears in all directory windows, always takes you back to the folder one level above the one that you're viewing. ♦

Running Programs from File Manager

In addition to helping you organize directories and files, File Manager allows you to start programs from its directory windows, just as you can from group windows in Program Manager. Experiment by starting one of the Windows tools:

1. Scroll the WINDOWS directory window until you can see the icon for NOTEPAD.EXE. This program is executed when you double-click the Notepad icon in Program Manager.
2. Double-click the NOTEPAD.EXE icon. File Manager loads Notepad and displays a blank Notepad window.
3. Close Notepad by choosing Close from the Control menu.

You can also use File Manager to load documents into the application that created them, by double-clicking the document icon just as you did in Program Manager in Chapter 2.

Organizing Directories and Files

Being able to start programs from File Manager is convenient, but the real strength of File Manager becomes apparent when you use it to organize your directories and files by moving, copying, and deleting them. Performing these operations by typing DOS commands is tedious and error prone. Not only do you have to pick the right command but you have to specify the right parameters in the right order—and type

---

Dictionary-style thumbing

To scroll quickly in a directory window, type the first letter of the name of the file you want to find. File Manager moves the window to display the first name in the list that starts with that letter. For example, typing *n* brings the first file whose name begins with *N* into view. ♦

Choosing commands from the Control menu

The Control menu is available in every File Manager window and is represented by the minus-sign icon in the window's top-left corner. To choose a Control menu command, click the icon to display the menu, and then double-click the command you want. From the keyboard, press Alt-Spacebar to access the Control menu. ♦

Window closing shortcut

To quickly close a window, double-click the Control menu icon in the window's top-left corner. If double-clicking doesn't work, click the icon to display the menu, and check that the Close command is available for that window. (It's not available for the Directory Tree window, for example.) If the command is available, try double-clicking even faster. ♦

everything without a single mistake. By using a visual interface to make common DOS operations less intimidating, Windows File Manager is following in the footsteps of the DOS shell released with DOS 4 and commercial shell programs such as Norton Commander.

Before you practice using File Manager to create directories and move files, you might want to take a short detour to discuss the basics of file-organization philosophy. If you have ever wasted time trying to locate a file, you might find that spending a few minutes now deciding how to avoid such incidents in the future will more than repay you in increased efficiency.

Deciding on a System

There are no hard and fast rules for organizing files, and the scheme you come up with will depend on the nature of your work. For example, the files of CityRock Gym (the sports club introduced in Chapter 2) are client-based, so it makes sense to identify the gym's files by client. CityRock might use a client's initials as the first two or three characters of the filename of every file connected with that account, follow these letters with a date, and use the extension to identify the type of file. For greatest flexibility a file-naming system should use all eight character spaces allowed by DOS and always use the same character to pad out empty spaces. The underscore (_) is a good choice. Thus, a filename such as RJR12210.LET might designate a letter written to a client

Starting Windows at the File Manager window

You can have File Manager (or any other program) load as soon as you start Windows, instead of Program Manager. Use Notepad to open the WIN.INI file from the WINDOWS directory. The third line of the file should be *RUN=*. Click an insertion point after the equal sign, type *winfile.exe* (the File Manager program file), and save the WIN.INI file. The next time you start Windows, Program Manager minimizes to an icon and File Manager opens, allowing you to use File Manager as your main base of operations. You can switch back to Program Manager at any time by double-clicking its icon. ◆

Naming files

DOS has an eight-character limit for filenames. This sometimes necessitates compromises in a file-naming system. In the example filenames in this chapter, the year is designated only by its last digit. For example, 1990 is designated by 0, and 1991 by 1. This system will cause confusion only if your active archives span more than a decade. ◆

whose initials are RJR on December 21, 1990, whereas the filename RJR01401.INV might designate an invoice sent to the same client a few weeks later.

The important thing is to come up with a simple scheme and to apply it consistently. In an eagerness to impose structure, people sometimes go overboard, developing convoluted naming systems and subdirectory mazes in which it is easy to get lost. The result is usually as bad as no system at all, because it is less hassle to create filenames on the fly and search a huge directory than it is to remember how the system works.

The advantage of a little filenaming discipline becomes apparent when you accumulate so many files in one directory that you need to create subdirectories to make the files more manageable. For example, suppose CityRock Gym decides to organize their files by type rather than by client. They could create a subdirectory called INV, select all the files in the large directory that have INV as their extension, and move all their invoice files with one command.

It's definitely worth coming up with a few simple rules for organizing directories and files and then training yourself to apply them consistently. You can then use File Manager to manipulate the files, both individually and in groups, as you'll see in the next section.

Associating extensions

Most documents from Windows applications are automatically associated with their parent applications. For example, if you double-click a TXT file in Program Manager, Notepad opens with the document in its window. Similarly, double-clicking a WRI file loads Write, and double-clicking a DOC file loads Microsoft Word for Windows. If you want a Windows application to open documents created by a different application, you must create an association between the documents' extensions and the Windows application.

To open only one document regardless of its extension, simply drag the document's icon over to the application's icon. This starts the application, which then attempts to open the document.

To permanently associate a particular extension with a program, click a file with the extension, and choose Associate from the File menu. Type the name of the program to which you want to associate the extension, and click OK. Of course, the application must be able to open or convert that particular document type for the association to work. ♦

Creating a New Directory

Earlier in the chapter, you displayed the WINDOWS directory window by double-clicking the WINDOWS folder in the Directory Tree window. Redisplay this directory window now so that you can follow along with the next exercise.

Although you can easily scroll the WINDOWS directory window and can even jump around in the list of files by typing letters on the keyboard, you may want to organize the WINDOWS directory to make it easier to find specific files. As you scroll the window, notice that the names of files that come with Windows follow a definite pattern. You may not know exactly what a file is or does, but you can tell that certain files relate to specific Windows accessories, such as the calculator, because they have the same filename (CALC). Other files probably perform similar functions because they have the same file extension. In this exercise, you are going to create a new subdirectory for all the Help files—those with HLP as their extension. After moving the Help files into a directory of their own, you will find it quicker and easier to locate program files in the WINDOWS directory window. Follow theses steps:

1. Choose the Tile command from the Window menu. The WINDOWS directory window and the Directory Tree window arrange themselves neatly on the screen.

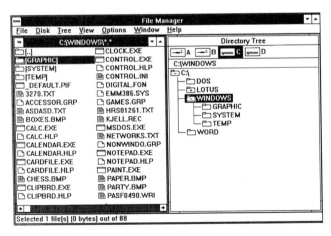

2. With the WINDOWS directory window active, choose the Create Directory command from the File menu. The Create Directory dialog box appears so that you can give the directory a name.

3. Check that the current directory is C:\WINDOWS. If it is not, click Cancel, and then click anywhere in the WINDOWS directory window to make it active before choosing the Create Directory command again.

4. In the Name text box, type *help*, and click OK. A new HELP folder appears both in the directory window and in the Directory Tree window.

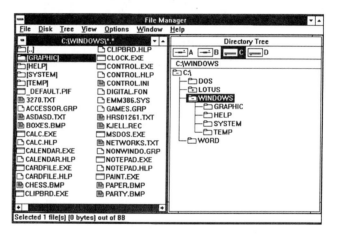

5. Again, check that the WINDOWS directory window is active. Then choose Include from the View menu. The Include dialog box appears, allowing you to specify the files you want displayed in the directory window.

Notice that by default all filenames (represented by *) and all extensions (represented by .*) are displayed.

You can restrict the display to files with certain characters in their names or in their extensions by changing this default setting. For this exercise, you want to restrict the display to files with the HLP extension.

6. Click an insertion point at the end of the default setting, and press Backspace to delete the second *.

7. Type *hlp*, and press Enter. The title of the directory window is now C:\WINDOWS*.HLP, and the window displays only files with the HLP extension.

8. Choose Select All from the File menu. All the files in the directory window darken to show they are selected.

9. Position the mouse pointer anywhere in the directory window and hold down the left mouse button. The pointer changes to a stack-of-documents icon. Still holding down the button, drag the mouse to the right until the icon is over the HELP folder in the Directory Tree window. A dotted rectangle surrounds the folder when the document-icon pointer is in the correct spot.

10. Release the mouse button. Click Yes to confirm the mouse action. Windows moves all the Help files from the WINDOWS directory into the HELP directory, displaying its progress in a message box. When the program has moved the files, it closes the directory window.

11. Double-click the HELP folder in the Directory Tree window. Verify that the HLP files are safely stored in their new directory, and then choose Close from the Control menu to close the HELP directory window.

Wildcards

The asterisk (*) and the question mark (?) are "wildcard" characters that allow you to select specific files. An * matches anything that follows it. A ? matches any single character. For example, *.INV matches all files with an INV extension, and RJR????0.INV matches all invoices sent to client RJR in the year 1990. ♦

The View menu

The View menu commands allow you to customize how files appear in a directory window. You can view files based on name, date, size, or file type. Choose the Include command to fine-tune the display even further. Experiment with these choices to find a configuration that works well for you. ♦

Confirmation settings

Choosing the Confirmation command from the Options menu lets you change confirmation settings. You may want to disable settings you find inconvenient. Despite the bother, leave the Confirm On Delete setting enabled. You will probably catch yourself, more than once, about to delete something you need. ♦

Telling Windows Where to Look for Files

Whenever you move files from the WINDOWS directory, you need to make sure that Windows knows where to find the files if you need to use them. When Windows was installed on your system, the Setup program added to your AUTOEXEC.BAT file directions for finding the Windows files. Because you have changed the location of the Help files, Windows will no longer be able to find them. Try this:

1. Choose Index from the Help menu. Windows displays the Help screen and then displays a message box announcing that it can't find the file it needs.

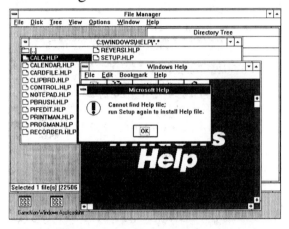

2. Click OK to close the message box, and then choose Close from the Control menu, or double-click the Control menu icon, to close the Help window.

AUTOEXEC.BAT	Batch files	Paths and the PATH command
AUTOEXEC.BAT is a special batch file that DOS automatically runs when you boot up your computer. The AUTOEXEC.BAT file typically contains system configuration commands, a PATH command, directions for how the DOS prompt will appear, and perhaps instructions to run a shell, or some other program you commonly use. ♦	Batch files are text files that execute a string of DOS commands. To create a batch file, type the DOS commands in a text file, with a carriage return at the end of each line, and save the file with the BAT extension. When you run the batch file from Windows, it quits to DOS, carries out the commands, and then returns to Windows. ♦	A file's path is its filename preceded by the drive, directory, and subdirectories (separated by \ signs) on which it is stored. The PATH command tells DOS where to look for files by giving their paths. If you don't specify a path, either directly or in the AUTOEXEC.BAT file, DOS "sees" only files located in the root directory. ♦

To tell Windows where to find the files, you will have to modify your AUTOEXEC.BAT file. Sound scary? Follow these simple instructions to load the file into the Notepad accessory and make the necessary changes.

1. In the Directory Tree window, double-click the WIN-DOWS folder to display the WINDOWS directory.
2. Type *n* to move to the files whose names begin with *N*, and locate NOTEPAD.EXE. If necessary, use the scroll bar arrows to bring it into view.
3. Double-click NOTEPAD.EXE to start Notepad. Windows starts the program and displays a blank Notepad window. You need to load the AUTOEXEC.BAT file into the window so you can work on it.
4. Choose Open from the File menu. Windows displays a dialog box so that you can enter the name of the file in the Filename box.

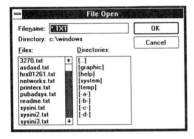

5. Press Backspace to erase *.TXT, type *.*bat*, and press Enter. Windows redisplays the Open dialog box, this time listing WINDOWS-directory files with the BAT extension. The AUTOEXEC.BAT file does not appear in the list because it is stored in the root (C:) directory, which is one level above the WINDOWS directory.
6. Double-click the [..] symbol at the top of the Directories list box to display root-directory files with the BAT extension in the root directory. Windows redisplays the Open dialog box, listing the BAT files.

7. Double-click AUTOEXEC.BAT. Windows closes the Open dialog box and loads the file into the Notepad window. To inform Windows of the existence of the newly created HELP directory, you need to add a new path to the PATH line. Then when you choose one of the commands on the Help menu, Windows will know to look in the HELP directory for the files it needs.

8. Use the arrow keys to move the cursor to the beginning of the PATH line, and then press the End key to move to the end of the line.

9. Type *c:\windows\help*.

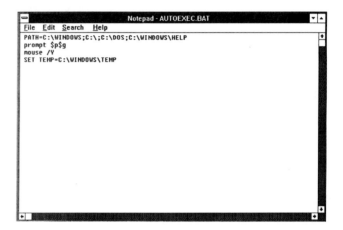

10. Choose Save from the File menu to save the new file without changing its name.

11. Choose Close from the Control menu to close Notepad.

The AUTOEXEC.BAT file is run only when you start your computer, so Windows won't know that you have modified the file unless you restart your machine. Do that now:

1. Simultaneously press the Alt, Ctrl, and Del keys to "reboot" your computer. (If your computer doesn't respond to this key combination, you will have to turn the power off and then on again.) Your computer runs the modified AUTOEXEC.BAT file and records the new PATH.

2. Restart Windows by typing *win* at the DOS prompt, and then double-click the filing-cabinet icon to load File Manager.

3. Choose Index from the Help menu. This time, Windows displays the Help screen and lists the topics about which help is available. Choose Close from the Control menu to close the Help window.

Moving Files to a Floppy Disk

Suppose you are running out of room on your hard disk and you are looking for files to remove in order to give yourself a little breathing space. For example, CityRock Gym might decide to remove all the invoice files for 1990, but they would almost certainly want to move the files into archival storage on a floppy disk rather than erasing them completely. If they have named all their invoice files consistently with names like RJR12040.INV, as we discussed earlier in the chapter, moving the files for 1990 is simple. You would first display all files whose names end in 0 and whose extensions are INV by choosing Include from the View menu and typing ???????0.INV in the Filename box. Then they would select all the displayed files and copy them to a floppy disk.

On your system you may not have a set of files with which you can practice moving files to a floppy disk, so use the Help files that you just moved into the HELP directory to follow along with this exercise:

1. In the Directory Tree window, click the WINDOWS folder to display its subdirectories, then double-click the HELP folder to display the HELP directory window.

Format Diskette

File Manager allows you to format disks, and even make bootable system disks, without quitting to DOS. Simply choose Format Diskette from the Disk menu, and select a floppy disk drive from the drop-down menu. Click OK, and then click Format when prompted by File Manager. In the next dialog box that appears, select or deselect the High Capacity option to format high-density or low-density disks. Select the Make System Disk option to create a bootable DOS disk. When File Manager has finished formatting the disk, it asks whether you want to format another disk. Click Yes to format another disk or No to quit. ◆

Moving vs. copying files

Here's how you move and copy files between directories on the same drive: Move by dragging; copy by holding down the Ctrl key while dragging.

Here's how you move and copy files between drives: Copy by dragging; move by holding down the Alt key while dragging. ◆

2. Choose the Tile command from the Window menu to arrange the Directory Tree window and the HELP directory window side by side.

3. Insert a blank, formatted floppy disk in drive A.

4. With the HELP directory window active, choose Select All from the File menu. Below the list of selected files, Windows reports how many files are selected and their total size in bytes. You may not have enough room to move all the files to one floppy disk, but for purposes of this exercise, just move as many as will fit.

5. Hold down the Alt key, and while holding down the left mouse button, drag the mouse until the stack-of-documents pointer is over the A: drive icon in the Directory Tree window. Release the mouse button. Windows begins moving Help files from the HELP directory to the disk in drive A, reporting on the progress of the move operation in a message box. If another box appears with the message that there is no more room on drive A, click OK.

6. When Windows has finished moving files, click the A: drive icon, and then double-click the A: folder, to display the list of files now stored on the disk in drive A.

Copying Files from a Floppy Disk

Now that you know how to quickly move files from your hard disk to a floppy disk, you'll want to know how to use

---

Other ways of selecting and deselecting files

To select a block of files, click the first file, then hold down the Shift key and click the last file in the block. Windows then selects the whole block of files.

To select files that are not adjacent in a list of files, click the first file, and then hold down the Ctrl key and click the next file. Continue holding down Ctrl and click-ing the files you want, until they are all selected.

The status bar at the bottom of the File Manager window tells you how many files you have selected and their collective size.

To deselect just one file from a group of selected files, hold down the Ctrl key and click the file you want to deselect. ♦

The Exit command

When you exit File Manager, a dialog box similar to the one that appears when you exit Windows appears. Click the Save Settings box to save any changes you may have made to the way File Manager displays files, and then click OK. ♦

File Manager to copy them back to your hard drive. Again, we'll use the Help files for demonstration purposes. The list of Help files on the A: drive should be open on your screen. Behind it you should see the HELP directory you created.

1. Choose Select All from the File menu.

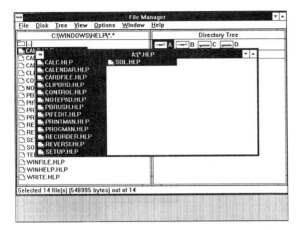

2. Hold down the left mouse button, drag the selected files in the A: folder into the HELP directory window behind, and release the button. You can release the files anywhere in the HELP directory window except in the [..] folder. If you drop the files there, they will be copied to the WINDOWS directory. Windows copies all the Help files from the disk in drive A into the HELP directory.

Notice that you did not hold down the Alt key while dragging this time. By default, Windows *copies* files from one drive to another. You need to hold down the Alt key only if you want to *move* the files. By contrast, when you drag files from one directory to another on the same drive, as you did when moving the Help files from the WINDOWS directory to the HELP subdirectory, the Windows default action is to *move* the files. You need to hold down the Ctrl key while dragging if you want to *copy* the files.

In this chapter, we have shown you a few basic file operations that will make your work with Windows more productive. In the next chapter, we look at more Windows techniques for improving efficiency: multitasking and sharing information among programs.

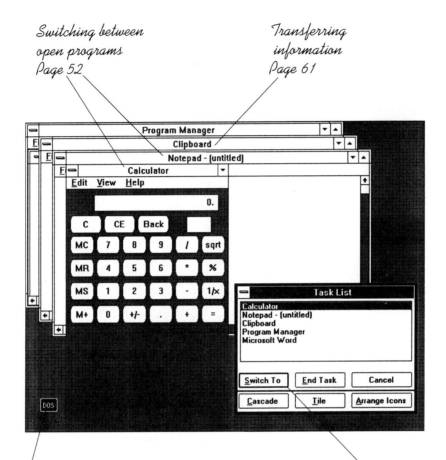

Switching between open programs
Page 52

Transferring information
Page 61

Non-Windows applications
Page 61

Another way to switch
Page 57

4

Switching and Sharing

Perhaps the single most important Windows feature is its ability to run more than one program at a time. Although being able to easily group programs visually and organize files logically will undoubtedly increase your efficiency, multitasking will probably be your main reason for working in the Windows environment.

In Chapters 2 and 3, you got a feel for moving among open windows and copying information from one to another. In this chapter, we cover switching from one program to another and sharing information among them in more detail. After reading this chapter, you'll begin to see how to take advantage of having a variety of programs at your fingertips.

Multitasking Techniques

The term *multitasking* may sound intimidating, but the concept is simple: Multitasking is running more than one program at the same time. All three Windows modes allow some degree of multitasking between Windows applications. For example, you might use the Terminal program to download a file from an online service while using the Notepad program to jot down notes for a meeting with a client. No longer do you have to wait for the communications program to finish before you can use the computer for other work.

Although you can have more than one program running at the same time, only one program can run *in the foreground*, meaning that its window is active and visible on the screen. Any other open programs run *in the background*, meaning that they are busy behind the scenes, either carrying out some prescribed task or waiting for your next instruction.

To see the difference between foreground and background applications, lets go back to CityRock Gym in Emeryville, California. Suppose Peter Mayfield wants to calculate the total number of hours worked the previous week by the staff. Learn how by following these steps:

1. Assuming that you have just started Windows and that the Program Manager window is open on your screen, double-click the Notepad icon to display an empty Notepad document.

2. Type the names of the staff members—*Hanneli, Amy, David, Bill, Mike,* and *Robin*—pressing Enter after each name.

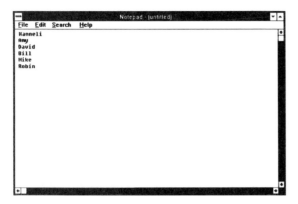

3. Double-click the Program Manager window to activate it. Because the Notepad window is no longer active, the window disappears into the background. However, Notepad is still running, and although you can't see it, the file with the list of staff names is still open.

4. Double-click the Calculator icon to run the Windows Calculator program. The image of a standard calculator appears on the screen.

5. Add the hours worked last week by the first staff member. For this example, click the 5 key, and then click the + key. Next, click 4 and +. Click 4 and + again.

Loading files into Notepad

Notepad can load unformatted ASCII files up to 50 KB in size. If lines of text go beyond the right border of a Notepad window, turn on Word Wrap so that all the text appears in the window. Turning on Word Wrap is for display purposes only; it doesn't affect the text file in any way. ◆

Entering numbers

You can use the keyboard instead of the mouse to enter numbers into Calculator. Just press the NumLock key on your keyboard and use the numeric keypad to enter numbers and operators. ◆

The scientific Calculator

Choosing Scientific from the View menu turns Calculator into a powerful, full-featured scientific/programmer's calculator. The basic algebraic functions remain, but you can also use this calculator to perform many different scientific and statistical calculations in either decimal, binary, octal, or hexadecimal number systems. ◆

Then click 6 and +. Finally, click 8 and +. The display bar shows the total: 27.

6. Choose Copy from the Edit menu. The contents of Calculator's display bar are copied to the Clipboard. Now you need to paste the total in the Notepad file. But where is the Notepad window, and how do you activate it?

7. Hold down Alt and press Esc. The Calculator window disappears, leaving only the Program Manager window on the screen.

8. Press Alt-Esc again. Notepad is brought to the foreground, with the staff-names document open.

9. Click an insertion point after the first staff member's name, press the Tab key, and choose Paste from the Edit menu. The total, 27, is pasted into the Notepad document.

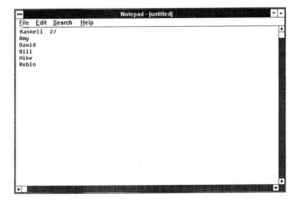

10. Now you need to go back to Calculator to total the second staff member's hours. Press Alt-Esc to activate Calculator, and type in some hours for Amy. Then choose Copy to put the total on the Clipboard.

11. Press Alt-Esc twice to bring Notepad to the foreground, click an insertion point after the second staff member's name, press the Tab key, and choose Paste to enter her total hours.

Finding Background Programs

When several programs are running at once, you may forget that a particular program is already running and double-click the program's icon in the group window to start it again. Usually, Windows reports that the program is already running and that you can run the program only once.

You may also have problems locating specific programs. As you've seen, one easy way to find a program is to cycle through all those that are open by pressing Alt-Esc. Here's another way to see at a glance which programs are running in the background:

1. Press Alt-Esc until the Program Manager window is active.

2. Click the Minimize button in the top-right corner of the Program Manager window. (You can also choose the Minimize command from the window's Control menu.) The Program Manager window shrinks to an

---

Running multiple copies of an application

Some applications can run several "copies" of themselves. For example, you could run a standard Calculator as well as a scientific Calculator, or run several Notepads, sharing information among them. To run multiple copies of an application, start the program as you would normally and then simply start it again. ♦

Alt-Esc

Pressing Alt-Esc brings open programs to the foreground one at a time, in the order in which you opened them. Because Program Manager was the first program Windows loaded, it comes to the foreground first. ♦

Background window maneuvering

If you have several programs running when you minimize Program Manager, some windows may obscure others. Drag some windows out of the way until you can see the program you need, and then activate its window. ♦

icon at the bottom of the screen, and Windows displays the windows of the programs that are running in the background—in this case, Notepad and Calculator.

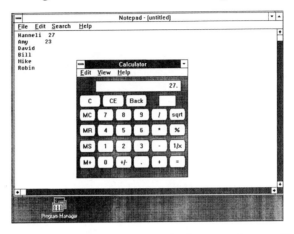

3. Click the Calculator window and use Calculator to total the hours of the third staff member, typing five numbers and adding them. Then choose Copy.

4. Click the Notepad window. Instead of disappearing, the Calculator window moves behind the Notepad window. (You may have to shrink your Notepad window to see Calculator.)

5. Click an insertion point after the third staff member's name, press the Tab key, and choose Paste to enter his total hours.

Minimizing Running Programs

You can minimize the windows of running programs so that they are represented by icons at the bottom of the screen. If you minimize a program while the Program Manager window is maximized, the program icons can be hard to find. But when Program Manager is also minimized, the icons are easy to spot, and you can click them to activate the programs. Try this:

1. Click the Minimize button in the top-right corner of the Notepad window. The window shrinks to an icon and moves to the bottom of the screen. The Calculator window is now active.

2. Use Calculator to total the fourth staff member's hours, choose Copy, and then click the Calculator window's Minimize button to shrink the window to an icon.

3. Now double-click the Notepad icon. The icon expands back to display the document window.

4. Click an insertion point after the fourth staff member's name, press the Tab key, and choose Paste to enter his total hours.

5. Click the Notepad window's Minimize button to send the window back to the bottom of the screen as an icon.

6. Double-click the Calculator icon to display Calculator, total the fifth staff member's hours, choose Copy, and click the Minimize button.

7. Activate Notepad, click an insertion point after the fifth staff member's name, press the Tab key, choose Paste to enter his total hours, and click the Minimize button.

Using Task Manager

The techniques that we've just discussed for finding and activating programs work well when you are running only a few applications at one time. However, when you are running many applications, especially non-Windows applications, you need a more efficient way of switching among them. Windows anticipates this need by providing a feature called Task Manager.

Task Manager shortcut

Double-click on any empty area of the desktop to display the Task List dialog box. Or press Ctrl-Esc. Remember, the desktop is the area behind all open windows and icons. If the Program Manager window is maximized, you can't see the desktop. ♦

Accessing Task Manager in non-Windows applications

When a non-Windows application is running full screen, no Control menu icon is displayed, so you cannot choose the Switch To command to access the Task List. However, you can still use the Ctrl-Esc shortcut. Windows temporarily switches to Program Manager and opens the Task List window. ♦

Task List is complete

If you are running more than one copy of the same program, each copy is listed in the Task List window, so you can, for example, select between an open standard Calculator and an open scientific Calculator. In addition, any open Windows-application documents are also listed, so you can, for example, select between two open Notepad documents. ♦

Activating programs from the Task List You access Task Manager by choosing the Switch To command, which is found on the Control menus of most program windows. Choosing Switch To opens the Task List window, which lists the running programs. Switching from one to another is then a simple matter of selecting the program you want to activate. Try using Task Manager to switch between Notepad and Calculator:

1. Double-click the Program Manager icon to expand its window.

2. Choose Switch To from the Control menu in the top-left corner of the Program Manager window to display the Task List. The open applications appear in the list box, with the active application—Program Manager— at the top of the list. The other two programs are listed in the order in which they were opened.

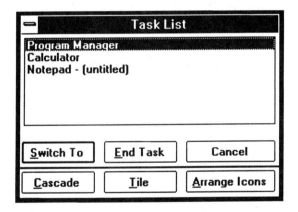

3. Click Calculator, and then click the Switch To button, or simply double-click Calculator (the shortcut), to activate the Calculator window.

4. Use Calculator to total the hours for the sixth staff member, Robin, and choose Copy.

5. Choose Switch To from the Control menu to display the Task List, and click first Notepad and then the Switch To button, or double-click Notepad. The Calculator window disappears. In the Notepad window, click an insertion point after Robin's name, press the Tab key, and choose Paste to enter her total hours.

6. Click anywhere in the Program Manager window to send Notepad to the background.

Quitting programs from the Task List   Using Task Manager, you can quit an open application without first switching to the program. To quit Calculator and Notepad:

1. Choose Switch To from the Program Manager's Control menu, and click Calculator to select it.
2. Click the End Task button. If no document is open, Windows closes the program and the Task List window.
3. Choose Switch To again. This time, click Notepad, and then click the End Task button. Because your Notepad document is open and has not been saved, Windows brings the Notepad window to the foreground and asks whether you want to save the document before quitting.

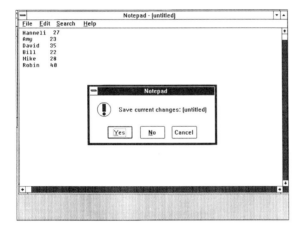

4. Click Yes. Windows displays the File Save As dialog box so that you can specify a filename.
5. Type a name like HRS01261.TXT (meaning *hours for the week ending January 26, 1991*) in the Filename box, and click OK. Windows closes the program and the Task List window.

Quitting non-Windows applications   In 386 Enhanced mode, you cannot quit a non-Windows application by clicking the End Task button. You must exit the application in the usual way. If you are running Windows in Real or Standard modes, when you click End Task to close a non-Windows application from the Task List window, Windows can't tell whether the application's active file has been saved, so it always warns you that the application is still active. If you are certain that you have saved the application's active file, simply click

OK in the message box to close the application. An unsaved file is lost when the application closes.

Arranging windows and icons with the Task List The Cascade, Tile, and Arrange Icons buttons in the Task List window work similarly to the commands with the same names on Program Manager's Window menu. (These commands were discussed in Chapter 2). The only difference is that these buttons affect all application windows and icons, whether they are running in the foreground or the background, except non-Windows applications that are running full screen.

Selecting Cascade in the Task List window causes open application windows (including Program Manager) to overlap so that the title bar of each window is visible. Selecting Tile arranges and sizes the windows so that none of them overlap. (Some windows, like the Calculator window, cannot be resized. As a result, they are unaffected by the Tile option, and the Cascade option cannot arrange them as neatly as other windows.) Selecting the Arrange Icons button arranges all open application icons neatly across the bottom of the screen. Note that these three buttons do not affect windows and icons within the Program Manager window; they affect the Program Manager window as a whole.

Non-Windows application switching	Non-Windows application icons	Quitting non-Windows applications
You can switch among open non-Windows applications by pressing Alt-Esc. If you are running Windows in Real or Standard mode, you see the message *Switching...* as Windows activates the next application. You don't see this message if you are running Windows in 386 Enhanced mode. ◆	All open non-Windows applications are represented by the standard gray DOS icon at the bottom of the screen, no matter what icon you assigned the program in Program Manager. ◆	Here is a brute-force technique for quitting non-Windows applications that are running in the background in 386 Enhanced mode. This technique should be used only in dire circumstances. Choose Settings from the application's Control menu, and click Terminate. Click OK when Windows displays a warning message. ◆

Multitasking with Non-Windows Applications

Because the amount of memory available in the three Windows modes varies, you can achieve different levels of multitasking in different modes. The real difference lies in how the modes handle non-Windows applications.

Real and Standard modes   Multitasking with non-Windows applications is not possible in Real and Standard modes. When you switch to a non-Windows application, any background applications are frozen, and background operations are not possible. The non-Windows application completely takes over the screen. When you switch to a Windows application or another non-Windows application, the current non-Windows application is halted.

386 Enhanced mode   In 386 Enhanced mode, you can run non-Windows applications either full screen or in their own windows, with a Control menu that gives them some of the functionality of Windows applications. You can run Windows and non-Windows applications in the background while running either a Windows or a non-Windows application in the foreground. The performance of all open programs may suffer slightly as Windows allocates "time slices" to each program.

Sharing Information among Applications

Another powerful Windows feature is the ease with which you can share information among applications. Sharing is accomplished by copying and pasting information between applications that use compatible data.

If you have followed along with the examples given so far, you know that sharing information among the programs that come with Windows is easy. Moving information between independent Windows applications, such as Word for Windows and Excel, is equally simple. Just select the data in the application file from which you're copying, choose Copy from the File menu, open the application file in which you want to paste the information, select an insertion point, and choose Paste from the File menu.

Sharing information with a non-Windows application can be more complicated, however, and you use different techniques in Real/Standard modes from those you use in 386 Enhanced mode.

Sharing in Real and Standard Modes

As a rule, our exercises are designed to show you how to use a particular Windows feature to accomplish some real task. Because it is not possible for us to predict which independent Windows and non-Windows applications you might want to work with, the instructions in the rest of this section are necessarily generic. They are, however, specific enough for you to apply them to the programs you use every day.

Copying from a non-Windows application   In both Real and Standard modes, you can copy only a full screen of text or numbers from non-Windows applications, because all non-Windows applications run full screen in these modes. The copy operation uses a character-based print-screen function, so you can't copy and paste graphics from a non-Windows application in these modes.

To copy a screenful of data from a non-Windows application to an open Windows application:

1. In the source file in the non-Windows application, display the information you want to copy, and press

---

Dynamic Data Exchange (DDE)

DDE is a Windows feature that allows some programs to automatically update pasted data. DDE creates a "hot link" between the source document and the document into which you pasted the data. For example, you can paste an Excel worksheet into a Word for Windows document in such a way that, whenever you change the

worksheet data, the Word document is updated correspondingly.

Windows reserves a portion of memory specifically to facilitate linking. Each application that is capable of using DDE has it's own way of creating the link. ♦

Running in the background

Windows programs and applications can run in the background in windows or as icons; full-screen non-Windows applications always run in the background as icons at the bottom of the screen. ♦

the PrintScreen key. (On older, non-enhanced keyboards, press Shift-PrtSc.) The characters on the screen are copied to the Clipboard.

2. Press Alt-Esc until the destination file in the Windows application is displayed.

3. Choose Paste from the Edit menu. The full screen, including menu names, window borders, and so forth, is pasted into the designated file. You will probably need to delete extraneous characters.

Pasting into a non-Windows application Pasting into a non-Windows application file is a little more complex than pasting into a Windows application file. Whether you are pasting information from one non-Windows application to another or from a Windows application to a non-Windows application, you can paste only unformatted text. Any other types of data and any text formatting is lost during the paste operation.

With the copied information from the Windows application or the non-Windows application already on the Clipboard, follow these steps to paste the information into a non-Windows application:

1. Switch to the destination document in the non-Windows application, and position the cursor where you want to paste the data.

2. Press Alt-Esc until the icon for the non-Windows application is selected at the bottom of the screen.

3. Click the icon. The application's Control menu drops down.

4. Choose Paste. The destination document in the non-Windows application is opened again, and the data is pasted, one character at a time, in the location of the cursor.

You can then format the data as necessary.

Sharing in 386 Enhanced Mode

In 386 Enhanced mode, if you run a non-Windows application full screen, you can use the copy and paste techniques just described for Real and Standard modes. However, if you run the application in a window, you can access Control-menu commands and have some of the functionality of a Windows application. For example, you can copy entire screens as bitmap (BMP) images and paste them into a Windows program such as Paintbrush. This technique allows you to copy a graphic or chart in a non-Windows application and use it in a Windows application.

By default, non-Windows applications will always run full screen, even in 386 Enhanced mode. To use the following methods to copy selected data or to copy the screen as a bitmap image, you need to run the non-Windows application in a window. To display an open application temporarily in a window:

1. Press Alt-Enter. The application appears in a window with a Control menu.

If you are running the program full screen in 386 Enhanced mode, you can also click the program's icon at the bottom of the screen to open its Control menu, choose the Settings command, and select the Window option.

To always run the non-Windows application in a window:

1. Open the program's PIF file with PIF Editor.
2. Choose the Windowed option.
3. Save the PIF file.

(PIFs and PIF Editor are covered in more detail on page 75).

Mouse limitations	**Selection strategy**	**Copying the screen**
When a non-Windows application is displayed in a window, the mouse does not work as it normally would. It simply acts as a selection tool. ♦	Select only the characters you want to copy. If your copy area includes window borders or menu names, these items are copied along with the selected text. ♦	Copying the screen is a way of sharing charts, drawings, and other images created in a non-Windows application. Press Alt-PrintScreen. The entire window, including borders, scroll bars, and menus, is copied to the Clipboard in bitmap (BMP) format. You can then paste the image into a paint program, manipulate it, and paste it into a Windows program. ♦

Copying from and pasting into a windowed non-Windows application Non-Windows applications running in windows have Control menus, just like Windows applications. Choosing Edit from this menu displays a submenu of editing commands, including Copy and Paste. To copy data from a windowed non-Windows application:

1. Use the mouse to select the data you want to copy by dragging through it.
2. Choose Edit from the Control menu, and then choose Copy from the Edit submenu to place a copy of the selection on the Clipboard.
3. Switch to the Windows or non-Windows application in which you want to paste the information, position the cursor, and choose Paste from the Edit menu or from the Control menu's Edit submenu.

This chapter covered some techniques that will make your Windows sessions faster and more productive. Now that you have an idea of the power of multitasking and you know some of the methods of sharing information among applications, we will move on to discuss the many useful programs that come with Windows. By opening various combinations of programs on your desktop, you can put Windows to maximum use in your daily work.

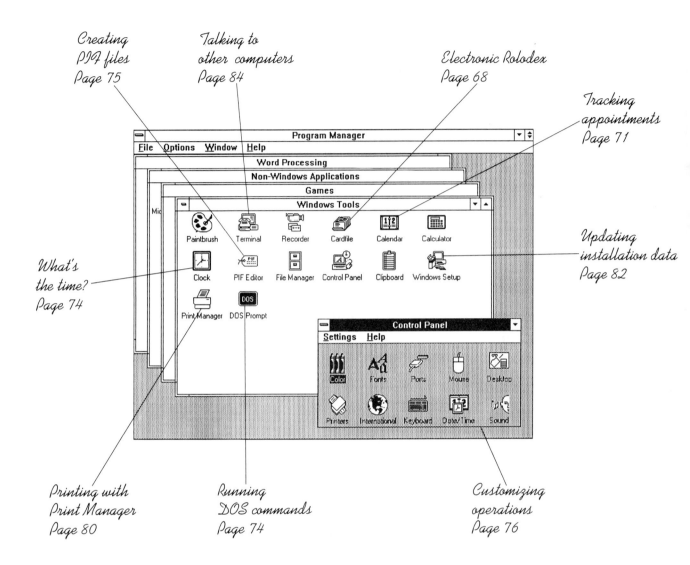

Creating
PIF files
Page 75

Talking to
other computers
Page 84

Electronic Rolodex
Page 68

Tracking
appointments
Page 71

What's
the time?
Page 74

Updating
installation data
Page 82

Printing with
Print Manager
Page 80

Running
DOS commands
Page 74

Customizing
operations
Page 76

5

The Windows Tools

Windows 3 comes with a grab bag of indispensable utilities and programs. If you've been following along with the exercises in this book, all these tools are in the Windows Tools group in Program Manager, except for Notepad and Write, which are in the Word Processing group that you created in Chapter 2. If you haven't been following along, you'll find the tools distributed between the Main and Accessories group windows. To start any Windows tool, simply double-click its icon.

Some of the Windows tools are quite large and involved, and others are quite small and simple. You'll use some of them often and others rarely, if ever. We introduced two useful tools, Notepad and Calculator, in Chapter 4. In this chapter, we first show you how to work with Cardfile and Calendar—electronic equivalents of your Rolodex and appointment book. Then we give you an overview of the other tools, finishing with an example of what you can do with Write and Paintbrush. Our goal is to tell you just enough to get you going and then let you experiment on your own.

Cardfile

You use Cardfile to keep track of addresses and phone numbers, or any similar sets of information, by recording the information on cards. Cardfile automatically alphabetizes the cards and, if you have a modem, can even dial the phone number on a card for you .

At CityRock Gym in Emeryville, California, Cardfile might be used to record the names and addresses of members. Here's how they might set up and use this handy tool:

1. Open Cardfile by double-clicking its icon in Program Manager. Cardfile opens with one blank card in its window. The card is divided into two areas: an index line (used for alphabetizing) at the top of the card, and an information area below it.

2. Choose Index from the Edit menu.

3. In the Index dialog box, type a member's name with the last name first (for example, *Miller, Jocelyn*), and click OK. Cardfile enters the name on the index line and moves the insertion point to the information area.

4. Type the address and phone number, pressing Enter when you need to start a new line. You can type up to 11 lines of text, and you can paste in unformatted text from other applications, such as Notepad and Write.

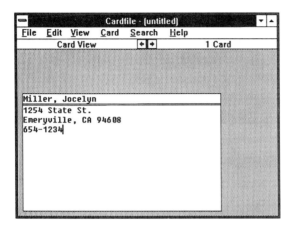

5. To add another card, choose Add from the Card menu.
6. In the Add dialog box, type the name you want to appear on the index line of the new card, and click OK. A new card appears on top of the first card, with the insertion point in the information area and the index line of the first card visible behind the new card.

Editing Cards

If you want to create a card that will be similar to a card you have already created, you can copy the existing card and then edit it. For example, here's how CityRock Gym would create a card for David Miller, Jocelyn Miller's husband:

1. With the card for Jocelyn Miller on your screen, choose Duplicate from the Card menu. An exact copy of the card appears in the window.
2. Double-click the index line, or choose Index from the Edit menu.
3. In the Index dialog box, select *Jocelyn* and press Del, then type *David*, and click OK.
4. Edit the text in the information area as necessary.

If you edit a card and want to return it to its previous state, before doing anything else—such as selecting another card—choose Restore from the Edit menu. Any changes you have made to the active card are undone.

If you want to delete a card, bring the card you want to delete to the top of the stack, and choose Delete from the Card menu. A dialog box asks you to confirm the command. Click OK, and Cardfile deletes the card.

Displaying Cards

Below the menu bar, Cardfile indicates how many cards are in the stack. The arrows to the left of the number of cards allow you to flip back and forth through the cards one at a time. To jump quickly to another card in the stack, simply click the card's index line to bring that card to the front of the stack.

If you have a large stack of cards, as CityRock Gym would have, you may want to display just their index lines, instead of complete cards. To see only the index lines, choose List from the View menu. List view shows an alphabetized list of the index lines of all the cards in the stack. To move to a particular card in the stack, click the index line of the card you want, and choose Card from the View menu. Cardfile switches back to card view, with the selected card at the top of the stack.

When you have accumulated a large number of cards, you can use menu commands to quickly display a specific card. For example, if the people at CityRock Gym want to display the address of a particular club member, they can choose GoTo from the Search menu and enter the member's name in the GoTo dialog box. (If they are uncertain of the spelling

Cardfile graphics

Any bitmap graphic created in a Windows paint program, such as Paintbrush, can be pasted onto Cardfile cards. Color graphics are converted to black and white. You can combine text and graphics. You can paste in a graphic of any size, but you can view only a card-sized section of it. Simply move the graphic to view other sections. ◆

Dialing numbers from Cardfile

If you have a modem, you can use Cardfile to dial the phone number on a card. Select the card, highlight the number, and choose Autodial from the Card menu. In the Autodial dialog box, make any adjustments necessary for automatic dialing, such as adding a prefix, and click OK. When the phone rings, pick up your phone and wait for an answer. ◆

Printing cards

If you want to use a Cardfile address database in a desktop Rolodex, you can print the database file on special perforated card stock. Use the settings in the Page Setup dialog box to align the addresses so that they print within the margins of the cards. ◆

of the name, they can enter just a part of it. And they don't need to worry about capital letters, because GoTo searches are not case sensitive.)

Suppose CityRock Gym wants to do a bulk mailing to all members in a certain ZIP code. To search the addresses in the information area, from card view they can choose Find from the Search menu and enter in the Find dialog box the numbers they want to search for. If Cardfile finds a match, it puts the matching card at the top of the stack and highlights the matching text.

Saving, Printing, and Merging

You save a Cardfile file the same way you save any other Windows file. Simply use the appropriate commands on the File menu. By default, Windows assigns a CRD extension.

You use the Print command on the File menu to print the card at the top of the stack in card view, and you use Print All to print all the cards in the stack, with three cards to a page. The cards are printed just as they appear in card view, with a border and an index line. See "Print Manager and Printing" on page 80 for more information.

You can join two saved Cardfile files to create one file by using the Merge command on the File menu. For example, CityRock Gym might want to combine a file of members' names and addresses with a file of vendors' names and addresses to create a list of people to whom they want to send season's greetings at the end of the year. To merge two files, you open one Cardfile file and choose Merge from the File menu. In the File Merge dialog box, you highlight the name of the file you want to merge into the open file and click OK. The cards from the two files are combined and alphabetized, and the card-count indicator reflects the new number of cards. If you want to keep the merged file, save it with a name that is different from those of both of the files from which it was created.

Calendar

You can use Calendar to remind yourself of important events at work or at home. Its alarm feature can even give you advance notice of appointments.

Calendar

Entering Appointments

At CityRock Gym, they might use Calendar to record appointments for prospective members to tour the facilities or to schedule special classes. To enter appointments:

1. Double-click the Calendar icon in Program Manager. A new, untitled Calendar window appears, with the current date and time at the top and an appointment area, divided into one-hour time intervals, below.

2. To make an appointment for Barry Scott at 3:00 PM this afternoon, click to the right of that time in the appointment area, and type *Barry Scott*.

3. In the notes area below the appointment area, type *Deadline for Climbing Magazine ad*. (You can use this area for any general notes for this date.)

You can change the one-hour time intervals to 15-minute or 30-minute intervals and the 12-hour format to 24-hour format, and you can change the 7:00 AM starting time. Simply choose Day Settings from the Options menu, and make the necessary changes. When you click OK, the appointment area will reflect your selections.

Suppose that Amanda Rawlings wants to tour CityRock Gym at 4:15 PM tomorrow. To display tomorrow's appointment area:

1. Click the right arrow at the top of the appointment area to move forward one day. The date above the appointment area changes to tomorrow's date.

2. To insert a special time slot in the appointment area without changing the one-hour format of the entire file, choose Special Time from the Options menu, type 4:15 in the Special Time text box, and click the PM button. Finally, click Insert. The new time slot is added to the appointment area.

3. Enter the appointment for Amanda Rawlings.

4. Click the left arrow at the top of the appointment area to move back to the calendar for today.

If Amanda Rawlings cancels her appointment and you need to delete the special time slot, you simply place the insertion point next to the time slot, choose Special Time from the Options menu, and click Delete.

Displaying Days and Months

Calendar allows you to display different days in a variety of ways. As you've seen, one way of navigating through a Calendar file is to click the left and right scroll arrows at the top of the appointment area. You can also use the commands on the Show menu. Choosing Today displays the current day, choosing Previous takes you back one day in the calendar, and choosing Next takes you forward one day. You can use the Date command to move quickly to a specific date.

You can display Calendar in month view rather than day view, either by choosing Month from the View menu or by double-clicking the date above the appointment area. The whole month is then displayed, with the date that was active in day view highlighted. The scroll arrows above the appointment area and the commands on the Show menu now move you through the Calendar file in months instead of days.

Setting Alarms

You can set alarms to remind you of important appointments, by using the commands on the Alarm menu. If you use alarms frequently, you should always work with Calendar running in the background; otherwise, the alarms can't sound. To set an Alarm, move the insertion point to the time at which you want to set the alarm, and choose Set from the Alarm menu. A small bell to the left of the time slot indicates that the alarm is set. When the time on your computer matches the alarm time, your computer beeps. If Calendar is running in the foreground, a dialog box displays any message you typed in the appointment area. If Calendar is running in a window in the background, the window's title bar flashes; if it is running as an icon, the icon flashes. Click the window or the icon to display the message.

You can use the Controls command on the Alarm menu to make all alarms go off from 1 to 10 minutes before the actual appointment time and to turn the alarm beep on and off.

Saving and Printing

Saving a Calendar file is similar to saving any Windows file. Just use the commands on the File menu. Calendar adds a CAL extension to saved files.

You can use the Print command to print the information that appears in the appointment and notes areas in day view; you can't print from the month view. Simply choose Print from the File menu, and specify in the From and To boxes the days with the schedules you want to print. When printing, Calendar skips over days and time slots that have no entries.

Clock

Clock

Clock

The simplest of the Windows tools, Clock has just one function: to tell the time in either analog or digital format. Double-clicking the Clock icon brings up a small window with a clock face on it. Use the Settings menu to switch between the analog and digital clock face. If you want to keep Clock open at all times, simply minimize its window to a clock-face icon that shows the current time.

The time Clock shows reflects your system time, which either is set by you each time you boot your computer or is held in memory by a battery. You can change the time using either DOS Prompt or Control Panel, both of which are discussed in this chapter.

DOS Prompt

DOS Prompt

DOS Prompt duplicates the MS-DOS command interface. You can use it to type in DOS commands, just as you would on the DOS command line, without leaving Windows. For example, you might use DOS Prompt to run a non-Windows utility, such as an archiving program that requires you to type many parameters on the command line to specify precisely the type of archiving you want.

To use DOS Prompt, double-click the DOS Prompt icon in Program Manager. The MS-DOS command line is displayed, looking as though you have left Windows and returned to DOS. But rest assured: You are still in Windows. Type the DOS command you need, just as you normally would. The program should run normally, though you may have trouble with some programs. When the program finishes running, the DOS command line is redisplayed. To return to Windows, type *exit*, and press Enter.

PIF Editor

When you ran the Windows Setup program, Windows created a Program Information File (PIF) for any non-Windows applications it recognized among the programs stored on your hard drive. Each PIF is a small settings file that helps Windows load the corresponding application by designating where the program is located and how much memory it requires.

PIF Editor

If Windows didn't recognize the program, chances are that you can create an icon for the program in Program Manager and it will run fine without a PIF. If it doesn't run properly, you need to use PIF Editor to write a PIF so that you can run the application from within Windows. It's not as hard as it sounds. Start by double-clicking the PIF Editor icon to open the PIF window, which looks like this:

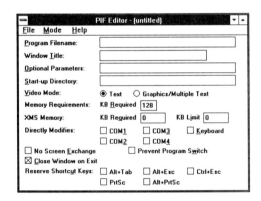

DOS Prompt no-no's	Quick start for programs	Default extensions
It's unwise to use utilities such as file-unerase or disk-defragmentation programs from DOS Prompt, because they can change the locations of files that Windows needs to operate properly. Always exit Windows to run these types of programs. ♦	In File Manager, you can double-click the PIF file of a non-Windows application to run the program. ♦	If you don't supply an extension, the following extensions are assigned to files you create with the Windows tools: Calendar: CAL Cardfile: CRD Clipboard: CLP Notepad: TXT Paintbrush: BMP Recorder: REC Terminal: TRM Write: WRI ♦

In the Program Filename box, type the path and filename of the non-Windows application. In the Window Title box, type the name you want for the application's icon in Program Manager. In the Optional Parameters dialog box, type any parameters you would normally enter to run the program from the DOS command line. (You can leave this box blank.) In the Start-Up Directory dialog box, type the name of the directory where the program is located. Finally, choose Save from the File menu and, in the File Save As dialog box, type the name of the program, adding a PIF extension. Then click OK.

Don't worry about the other options in the PIF Editor window for now. The next step is to link the PIF to the application's icon. Follow the process described on page 30 for creating a document icon.

After you have created the icon, you can double-click the icon in Program Manager to start the application. Depending on the mode you are running Windows in, the application may work and look a bit different than usual. If it crashes or misbehaves in any way, you can try to adjust the PIF to correct the problem. (See the Windows documentation for more information about setting specific options in the PIF Editor window.) Then start PIF Editor again, and open the PIF for the application so that you can change the settings.

Control Panel

Control Panel

Control Panel allows you to control how Windows runs and looks on your computer. This is the window displayed when you double-click the Control Panel icon in Program Manager:

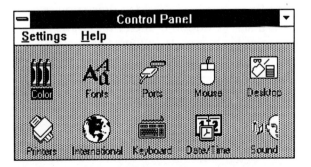

The icons in the window function like program icons, but they can't be moved, copied, or deleted. Following is a brief description of these options.

Color

The Color option allows you to set the colors of many of Windows' standard elements, such as scroll bars and the active title bar. You can select a preset color scheme or you can design one of your own. When you click the Save Scheme button and click OK, your color changes are immediately reflected on the Windows screen. Playing with colors can be fun, and we encourage you to experiment a bit with this feature to learn more about it.

Printers

The Printers option allows you to install another printer or to change the configuration of your current printer.

Fonts

The Fonts option allows you to add screen fonts to Windows for use with applications, such as Write and Microsoft Word, that make use of WYSIWYG (What You See Is What You Get) fonts. These fonts allow you to see text as it will look when it is printed. When you install a printer, screen fonts corresponding to the printer's fonts are automatically installed. If you buy additional fonts, you may want to use the Fonts option to install the accompanying screen fonts as well.

International

The International option allows you to select a country and automatically change settings such as the measurement system and date, time, and currency formats, to reflect those used in that country. You can also change these formats individually. You also use the International option to specify the language you want to work in. Windows then uses that language in all its dialog boxes, warnings, and so on.

Ports

The Ports option allows you to configure the communications setting for your computer's serial ports. The serial ports are used for external devices such as printers and modems.

To make identical settings to several ports, simply hold down the Shift key and click each port icon before changing the settings in the Setting dialog box. The changes you make will be applied to all the ports you selected, without you having to open multiple dialog boxes.

Keyboard

The Keyboard option sets the rate at which keys repeat themselves when held down. You select a speed from Slow to Fast on the Key Repeat Rate scroll bar in the Keyboard dialog box. Click the Test Typematic box to position the insertion point, and then hold down any character key to test the key repeat rate. Adjust the speed to suit your typing style.

Mouse

The Mouse option sets your mouse tracking speed and double-click speed. It also switches the function of the left and right buttons. For both tracking speed and double-click speeds, you select a speed from Slow to Fast on a scroll bar. Tracking speed is the distance the pointer moves compared with the distance the mouse moves. A fast tracking speed means the pointer moves a long way on the screen when you move the mouse a comparatively short distance on your desk. Double-click speed is the rate at which you must double-click an icon or a list item to activate it. A fast double-click speed means you must double-click very quickly. Unless you drink a lot of coffee, it's probably best not to set the double-click speed at its fastest setting. Use the TEST button below the Double Click Speed scroll bar to try out a new double-click speed. The button toggles from white to black or from black to white when you double-click it at the correct speed.

The Swap Left/Right Buttons option does just what it says. If you are a southpaw, and find it easier to click, highlight text, and so on, with the right mouse button instead of the left, select this option. The switch takes place immediately, so use the right mouse button to click OK and exit the Mouse dialog box.

Date/Time

The Date/Time option sets the system date and time, just as the DOS Date and Time commands do. Simply select the number you want to change in the Date & Time dialog box, and type in a new one. You can also select the numbers and click the up and down arrows to change the numbers. Note that the Date & Time dialog box reflects the date and time format set in the International dialog box.

Desktop

The desktop is the surface behind all windows, window icons, and minimized program icons. Think of it as the screen that Windows uses to block out the DOS command line. The Desktop option allows you to change the default solid pattern of the desktop, use a bitmap graphic as desktop "wallpaper," set icon and window spacing, and set the cursor blink rate.

To change the background pattern, select another pattern from the Name drop-down list. Click the Edit Pattern button to bring up a dialog box that lets you edit the pattern, create your own pattern, and remove patterns from the list.

You can also use any bitmap graphic file in the Windows directory as wallpaper. The default wallpaper is None. Windows comes with several bitmap images you can use for wallpaper, or you can create your own using Paintbrush. Choose the wallpaper graphic file from the File drop-down list, and select Center to place the graphic in the middle of the desktop, or Tile to fill the entire desktop with tiled copies of the graphic. (Using Tile or using a very large graphic obscures any desktop pattern you have chosen.)

Icon Spacing lets you set the distance that appears between icons when you choose the Arrange Icons command. Normally, the spacing set by Windows is adequate, but if you want more or less space between icons, use this option to change the setting.

The Sizing Grid settings, Granularity and Border Width, determine how windows are placed on the desktop and how window borders appear. The Granularity setting creates an invisible grid with which windows and icons align. The default Granularity setting is 0, or no grid. Making this setting greater than 0 can help keep your desktop neat, but also prevents you from placing an icon anywhere that doesn't align with the grid. The Border Width setting determines the width of window borders. The default is 3. If, when resizing windows, you find this border too thin to easily grab, you can make the Border Width setting larger.

The Cursor Blink Rate sets the speed at which the text insertion point blinks in any Windows program or dialog box that uses text. If the insertion point doesn't blink fast enough to catch your attention, you can use this setting to increase the blink speed.

Sound

The Sound option allows you to turn the computer's warning beep on and off. By default, the beep is on. Simply click the Warning Beep option in the Sound dialog box to turn it off.

386 Enhanced

The 386 Enhanced option controls how Windows handles multitasking applications when running in 386 Enhanced mode. The Device Contention settings affect how Windows reacts when a multitasking non-Windows application and a Windows application attempt to access the same serial port. You can select between three options for each serial port on your computer: Always Warn, Never Warn, and the default, Idle.

The Scheduling and the Minimum Timeslice settings both determine the processing time Windows devotes to each multitasking application. These settings, along with the Device Contention settings, are very technical, and definitely not for the novice to play with. Microsoft recommends that you accept the default settings.

Network

If you are working on a network, the Network icon appears in the Control Panel window. See the notes in Appendix B about using Windows on a network.

Print Manager and Printing

Print Manager

When you ran Setup to install Windows for the first time, you probably indicated the type of printer you intended to use. You follow the same basic procedure to print from all Windows tools and applications.

The first step is to choose Printer Setup from the File menu. In the Printer list of the Printer Setup dialog box, click the name of the printer you want to use. If you need to configure the printer for this print job, click the Setup button, make the changes in the dialog box that appears, and then click OK.

Next, choose Page Setup from the File menu. In the Page Setup dialog box, you can set margins and create a header and a footer for your file, using the following codes:

Code	Function
&d	Inserts today's date.
&t	Inserts the current time.
&p	Inserts the page number.
&l	Left aligns the header or footer.
&r	Right aligns the header or footer.
&c	Centers the header or footer.

You can combine these codes to make custom headers and footers. For example, if you want this footer in a printed Notepad file:

Meeting Notes   4/12/91   Page 1

enter this in the Footer text box:

&lMeeting Notes&c&d&rPage &p

When you have set up your pages, click OK. Then choose Print from the File menu. When you click OK, the file is either sent directly to the printer or is spooled (fed) to the printer by Print Manager. If you are not using Print Manager, wait for the file to finish printing before resuming your work.

Print Manager is Windows' built-in print spooler, which spools the file to the printer in the background while you carry out another task in the foreground. When you choose the Print command, Print Manager runs as a minimized icon

Print Manager Priority

The Low Priority, Medium Priority, and High Priority commands on the Print Manager Options menu dictate how fast files are printed and the extent to which Print Manager slows down the operation of foreground applications. Medium Priority is the default. Low Priority causes Print Manager to print more slowly but allocates more memory to foreground applications. If your foreground application runs too slowly while you are printing, try choosing Low Priority. If you have a very fast computer and the foreground application doesn't seem to be unduly affected by Print Manager, try choosing High Priority to speed up background printing. ♦

Printing on a network

If you are on a network, you may want to turn Print Manager off, because most networks have built-in print spoolers. Leave it on if you want to be able to view the names of files you have sent to the printer. ♦

and then closes itself when it has sent the last file in its list, or queue, to the printer.

If you are in the middle of printing several files and need to view or change the print queue, double-click the Print Manager icon. The Print Manager window appears, listing the printers you are connected to and the files in the queue. The file that is currently printing has a small printer icon next to it, and other files have a number to the left of their names, indicating their position in the queue. You can change the order of files in the queue, remove files, temporarily halt printing, and specify the distribution of memory between background printing and foreground application operations.

Windows Setup

Windows Setup

You use Windows Setup when you want to reconfigure one of the settings you made when you first installed Windows. For example, if you change your monitor, keyboard, mouse, or network software after you have installed windows, select Change System Settings from the Windows Setup dialog box. Select new settings as appropriate from the Display, Keyboard, Mouse, and Network drop-down lists, and insert any disks Windows prompts you for.

You can also use Windows Setup to install program icons in Program Manager. For example, if you acquire a disk full of public-domain utilities, choose the Set Up Applications command from the Windows Setup dialog box, and select the drive containing the new programs. Windows lists all applications it recognizes on the selected drive, including any for which you already have icons. Select the programs that need icons, and Windows creates them, putting them in either the Non-Windows Applications group window, or the Windows Applications group window. If Windows doesn't recognize a program, you'll need to manually create an icon for it in Program Manager (see page 30).

Windows Help

Although no icon appears for it in Program Manager, Windows Help is an application in its own right. A Help menu appears in every Windows application for which a Help file exists. Using Help is pretty intuitive, but it's easy to overlook a couple of useful features.

Choosing Annotate from Help's Edit menu displays a small text window in which you can add a note to the current Help topic for future reference. When you click OK to close the window, a small paper clip icon appears next to the topic name. Just click the icon to display your note.

The Bookmark feature lets you add bookmarks to Help files so that you can move to often-used places quickly. To mark a section, choose Define from the Bookmark menu. Either accept the default bookmark name (the name of the current section), or type your own name. When you click OK, the name appears in the Bookmark menu. You can then choose the bookmark to move directly to that spot in the file.

Recorder

This simple recorder program records a sequence—called a macro—of commands, actions, and characters that you enter using the keyboard or the mouse, so that you can reproduce the sequence by pressing a shortcut key. Recorder is best used for simple repetitive tasks, such as entering a closing to a letter or formatting selected cells in a spreadsheet program.

Recorder

To create a macro, open Recorder, and choose the Record command to display the Record Macro dialog box, which lists various options that tell Recorder how to record the

---

Recording mouse actions	**Macros can't be edited**	**Nested macros**
Macro programs are notoriously unreliable when it comes to recording complex, exacting mouse movements. For example, you can't record a Paintbrush session and then expect Recorder (or any other macro program) to recreate your masterpiece. Whenever possible, use the keyboard equivalent for any mouse action. ♦	Think through the macro ahead of time. Any mistakes you make will be recorded. You can change many of the settings you made in the Record Macro dialog box, such as the macro's shortcut key, name, description, and playback options, by selecting the macro's name and choosing the Properties command. But you can't modify the macro itself. ♦	You can nest macros up to five layers deep by pressing a macro's shortcut key while recording another macro. Of course, the macros must be in the same open file for nesting to work. ♦

macro and how to play it back later. You may need to experiment with different settings before your macro will record and run correctly. When you click Start to begin the macro recording session, Recorder minimizes to a blinking icon, indicating that it is recording. Switch to the program in which you want to record the macro, and perform the task you want to record. When the task is complete, switch back to Recorder, and either save the macro, resume recording, or cancel recording in the dialog box that appears. Finally, switch to Recorder again, and choose Save As from the File menu to save the macro for future use.

You can record many macros in a single Recorder file, and you can merge Recorder files using the Merge command. To run a macro, open the saved Recorder file, open the program that the macro runs in, and press the assigned shortcut key. (You can also run the macro by selecting it in the Recorder window or by choosing the Run command.) Recorder minimizes to an icon and plays back the macro. You can cancel a macro in progress by pressing Ctrl-Break.

Terminal

Terminal

Terminal is a full-featured telecommunications program that allows you to connect your computer via modem to online services, bulletin boards, and other computers. After you have connected your modem, use the commands on the Settings menu to set the baud rate, transfer protocal, and parity. Then use the Dial command to dial phone numbers, and use the commands on the Transfers menu to upload (send) and download (receive) files. To transfer a file while working in another program, make Terminal active, begin the transfer, minimize Terminal to an icon, and then switch back to the other program. When the transfer is complete, the computer beeps and the Terminal icon flashes. Simply activate Terminal to finish the online session.

If you use Terminal often, you will want to create macros so that you can carry out common procedures, such as logging on or off a service, by clicking buttons at the bottom of the Terminal window. Choose the Function Keys command on the Settings menu to bring up the Function Keys dialog box, in which you can enter eight macros. If you fill up the eight macro slots, you can select another level to display another eight slots. A total of four macro levels allows you to create up to 32 macros. You use these control codes to write macros:

Code	Function
^A–^Z	Sends control codes A through Z to the remote computer. Common control codes are ^H (backspace), ^J (line feed), and ^M (carriage return).
^$D<##>	Pauses for ## seconds before continuing the macro.
^$B	Sends a break code.
^$C	Dials the phone number you entered using the Dial command.
^$H	Hangs up the phone.
^$L1–^$L4	Changes to another macro level.

For example, this macro logs on to the GEnie online service:

    ^$C^$D03HHH^M^$D02xth4209,antwerp^M

The macro dials a predefined phone number, pauses for 3 seconds, types a user name and a carriage return, pauses for 2 seconds, and then types a password and a carriage return.

Using combinations of control codes, you can come up with some slick macros, but usually macros perform simple, repetitive tasks, such as logging on or off a service. Remember to give each macro a descriptive name and to save the Terminal file so that your macros are available for future use.

Dialing macros

If you get tired of using the Phone Number dialog box each time you want to dial a different number, create a set of macros to dial numbers you use often. Preface the number with all the necessary modem commands. For example, you could create the following macro to dial a number on a Hayes-compatible modem hooked up to a touch-tone phone system:

ATDT5551212^M.
Remember to include a carriage return to send the command.

Turn on Local Echo in the Terminal Preferences dialog box to see the command displayed on the screen. ♦

Macro buttons

As long as the Keys Visible box is checked in the dialog box, the macros you define appear as buttons at the bottom of the Terminal window. To cycle through the four levels of macros, click the Level button in the bottom-right corner. To use a macro, click its button. ♦

Write and Paintbrush

Next, we'll give you a taste of the power of the Windows Write and Paintbrush applications by discussing how you might use them to create a document. Our intent here is not to give you detailed instructions, but to give you an idea of what you can do with these applications. If you are familiar with word-processing and paint programs, you'll soon figure out these Windows applications by playing around with them.

For our example document, we've recreated a version of the Grand Opening announcement for CityRock Gym. The finished piece is a 5-by-4-inch postcard.

To create the announcement, we first double-clicked the Paintbrush icon in Program Manager to open the Windows paint program. Using the Curve tool (which draws arcs), the Line tool, the Paint Roller, and the Text tool, we created CityRock's logo, a stylized climber. We then used the Line and Text tools to create a map giving directions to the club:

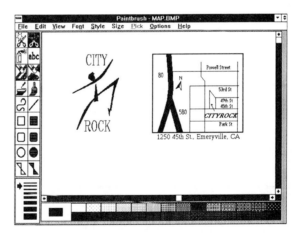

We placed the two graphics side by side and, after selecting them both with the Pick tool, we copied them to the Clipboard. We chose Save As from the File menu and saved the graphics with the filename LOGO-MAP. Because we didn't specify a directory and filename extension, the graphic document was saved in the WINDOWS directory and was given the extension BMP (for *bitmap*), which indicates that the file was created by the Paintbrush program. Then we chose Exit from the File menu to quit Paintbrush.

In Program Manager, we double-clicked the Write icon to open the Windows word-processing program. We immediately chose Paste from the Edit menu to insert a copy of the logo and map at the top of the blank document window, and then chose Move Picture to center them. We keyed in the text of the announcement, without worrying about formatting, and then started experimenting. We set margins, indents, and tabs by moving icons on the ruler at the top of the Write window, and we chose different fonts, sizes, and styles from the Format menu, until we were satisfied with the results.

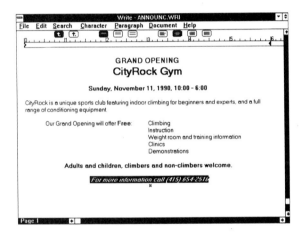

Next, we chose Save As from the File menu and saved the document with the name ANNOUNCE. The file was automatically given the extension WRI to indicate that we created the document in Write. Finally, we printed the document by choosing Print from the File menu. This is the final result:

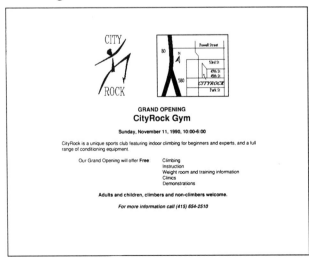

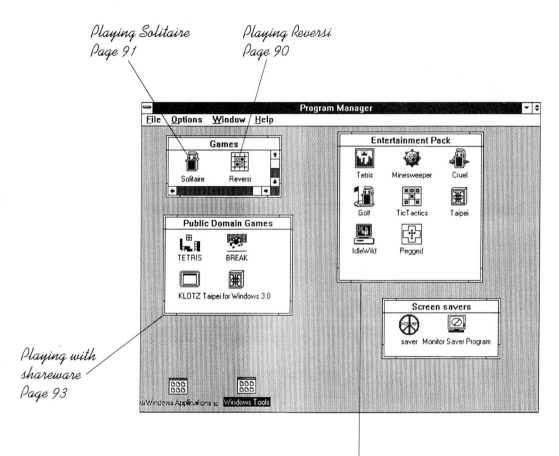

*Playing Solitaire
Page 91*

*Playing Reversi
Page 90*

Program Manager

File   Options   Window   Help

Games

Solitaire   Reversi

Entertainment Pack

Tetris   Minesweeper   Cruel

Golf   TicTactics   Taipei

IdleWild   Pegged

Public Domain Games

TETRIS   BREAK

KLOTZ   Taipei for Windows 3.0

Screen savers

saver   Monitor Saver Program

Windows Applications   Windows Tools

*Playing with
shareware
Page 93*

*Having fun with
Windows Entertainment Pack
Page 93*

6

Playing with Windows

Although most of the software that comes with Windows is designed to make you more productive, two programs—Reversi and Solitaire—are strictly for fun. Both are well-crafted versions of classic games. If you're waiting for a program to finish running, you can relax for a few minutes by playing one of these games in the foreground as the program finishes in the background.

The only mention made in the Windows documentation of these games is in the index, which refers you to the Help file for information. We'll take a few minutes to discuss basic rules and strategies, and then leave you to pit your wits against the computer.

Reversi

Reversi

Reversi is a variation of the Japanese boardgame Go and the commercial board game Othello. Like all games that have stood the test of time, this one is simple to learn and difficult to master. Start the game by double-clicking the Reversi icon in the Games group window.

Playing Rules

The object of the game is to dominate the 64-square board with your pieces. You play with red circles (white on a monochrome monitor) and the computer plays with blue circles (black on a monochrome monitor). Four pieces, two red and two blue, are on the board at the beginning of the game. You start the game by clicking an empty square to place a new red piece on the board. Your goal is to place the circle in such a way that you trap a blue circle between two red circles. Trapped pieces change to the opponent's color. If you are lucky, you can trap several pieces in more than one direction at one time. When neither player can make a move, the game is over, and the player with the most pieces on the board wins.

Tactics

A basic winning tactic is to position yourself at the edges of the board. Corners are critical positions; occupy them as quickly as possible! After a piece has been placed on a corner square, its color cannot be changed. If at all possible, avoid positioning circles on the squares adjacent to edge and corner pieces, but try to maneuver the computer into occupying these squares. Naturally, the computer is using these tactics as well, so plan your moves in advance.

Solitaire

Solitaire has many versions. Windows Solitaire is based on the card game Klondike (also known as Fascination and China-Man). It is as much fun to look at as it is to play, with twelve beautifully colored decks to choose from. The computer serves as dealer and scorekeeper. Start the game by double-clicking the Solitaire icon in the Games group window.

Solitaire

Playing Rules

When you start Solitaire, you see this layout, with the deck in the top-left corner, the four foundations to the right of the deck, and the seven columns of the tableau below them:

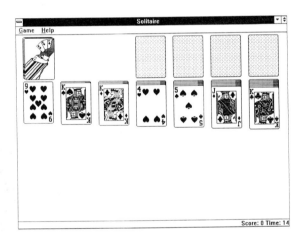

The computer deals 28 cards from the deck into the tableau, with the number of cards in the seven columns increasing from one to seven from left to right. The top card of each column is face up, the rest face down. When the scoring and timekeeping options are selected (as they are by default), Score and Time appear in the bottom-right corner of the window.

The object of the game is to use all the cards in the 52-card deck to build four stacks in the foundation. Each stack must contain all the cards from one suit (diamonds, clubs, hearts, and spades) in ascending sequence from ace to king. Only aces can be moved to an empty foundation, and only the next higher card of the same suit can be added to the foundation. Only kings can be moved to an empty column of the tableau.

Cards are dealt from the deck to the tableau, where you build columns of cards in descending sequence from king to ace in alternating suits. For example, you can put only the 5 of hearts or diamonds (red suits) on the 6 of clubs or spades (black suits). You can move the lowest face-up card in a column to the appropriate suit foundation if the card value is the next in ascending order for that suit.

You can move the face-up cards in a column as a single unit or individually to another column, as long as you maintain color sequence and descending card values. You can then turn over a face-down card uncovered by the move. If you move all the cards from one column to another column, you can move a king or a sequence of cards headed by a king to the empty column.

You turn over the next card in the deck, or turn over the top card in a face-down pile, simply by clicking the card with the mouse. You move a card between the deck, the tableau, and the foundations by dragging it and releasing the mouse button when the card reaches its destination. To move an entire face-up pile of cards, you position the mouse pointer on the highest card in the pile and drag the pile. To move a single card to a foundation, you can double-click the card instead of dragging it.

When you have turned over all the cards in the deck and want to make another pass through the deck, click to the left of the pile of turned-over cards. The pile returns to the deck area so that you can make another pass through it.

To pause during the game, click the Minimize button. Solitaire stops its scoring clock until you resume the game. The icon for the minimized Solitaire window appears as a card in a deck, with the currently selected card pattern.

Tactics

An out-and-out win in Solitaire is pretty hard to come by, but here are a few tips for better play and higher scoring. Obviously, if you're playing a timed game, you don't want to waste any time. Be cautious, but quick. And if you are playing the game with Draw One selected in the Options dialog box, keep your passes through the deck to a bare minimum, because each pass after the first entails a 100-point penalty. Although you can't cheat per se, when you get frustrated you can peek at the next card in the deck and then use the Undo command.

Other Diversions

The two games that come with Windows are fun, but you may find yourself looking for other diversions after a while. When Windows was first released, commercial games for the Windows environment were pretty scarce until Microsoft released the Windows Entertainment Pack, a great collection of games that would be at home on any Windows user's computer.

Windows Entertainment Pack

All the Entertainment Pack games make great use of color and 3-D shading. Unfortunately, the games come with no documentation other than advice to use the online help. Here's a look at the components of the Entertainment Pack.

Tetris   A nice color version of the Russian puzzle game. You use the keyboard to arrange falling blocks so that they don't fill the screen. The object: to play forever! Although you can't use the mouse to play the game, you can go head-to-head with another player in two-player mode, and you can choose from ten skill levels.

Taipei   A beautiful, full-color version of the Chinese board game Mah-Jongg. You remove colored tiles in pairs until none remain. Sounds simple, but the game can be maddening. This version has many nice features, including online hints, undo, autoplay, and seven tile configurations. It lacks several features of the older, public-domain version of the game, which is described later.

Cruel and Golf   Two fairly simple solitaire card games to play when you get tired of playing the version that comes with Windows.

Minesweeper   A particularly tough strategy game that can be nerve-wracking. You have to locate hidden "mines" on a grid without being blown up. You can play at three increasingly difficult skill levels and design a custom mine field.

TicTactics   Tic-Tac-Toe meets Mr. Spock! Play the regular 3x3 grid game (ho-hum), the 3x3x3 version, or the deadly 4x4x4 version. You can choose beginner, intermediate, or expert modes for each level. This game is entertaining but suffers because of an awkward perspective, which may lead to incorrect moves.

Pegged   Also known as Peg Solitaire. You remove marbles from a cross-shaped grid by jumping them checker-style. The object is to end up with one peg, preferably in the center of the grid. Seven progressively difficult levels of play are available.

Idlewild   Not a game, but a screen-saver utility, used to prevent the screen image from burning into your monitor or to instantly blank the screen from snooping eyes. Some people argue that screen savers aren't necessary and eat up memory, but this one is pretty to look at. Idlewild can present a fireworks show, a galaxy of shooting stars, and several other images, either at preset times or when you move the mouse into a corner of the screen.

Other Sources of Games

Some programmers are releasing games to the public as "freeware" or as "shareware." (The latter is sold for a nominal fee.) You can either write to the authors for copies or download them from software libraries on online services, such as GEnie and Compuserve or on local bulletin boards. Here is a list of a few of the very best games available:

Taipei   The public-domain version of the game released with the Windows Entertainment Pack. For some reason, several great features from this version have been omitted from the Entertainment Pack version, including a resizeable screen, adjustable difficulty settings, and the ability to make tile edges darker and lighter (crucial on some screens). The author requests $10 for a copy of this game, and it's well worth it. Write to the author, David Norris, at 17911 N.E. 101st Ct., Redmond, WA 98052.

Klotz An addictive clone of Tetris, in which you arrange falling blocks of different shapes. This version has many nice touches, including an active bar graph that rates your performance as you play. The author, Wolfgang Strobl, suggests you send $20 for a copy of the game. Write to him at Argelanderstr. 92, D-5300 Bonn 1, FRG.

Tetris Another Tetris clone. This one even sports the trademarked name. You can use the mouse as well as the keyboard to arrange the falling colored blocks in this version. The author requests $5 for this game. Write to Gary Kipnis, 78 Glenhill Ct., Fremont, CA 94539.

Screen Peace A far better screen-saver utility than the one in the Windows Entertainment Pack. A clone of the Macintosh screen saver Pyro!, Screen Peace can turn your screen into an aquarium, a fireworks show, and many other colorful, customizable images. This one is too beautiful to pass up, especially because it's "charity ware"; the author, Anthony Anderson, suggests a $5 or $10 donation, with proceeds going to charity. Write to the author at 1211 S. Quebec Wy. #3-108, Denver, CO 80231.

Appendix A
Notes about Installation

Setup, the Windows installation program, guides you pain-lessly through the entire process of getting Windows onto your computer. Setup also customizes Windows for your specific computer configuration. If Windows is not yet in-stalled on your system, read this appendix to be sure that you have the right equipment and that you know the answers to the questions Setup will ask.

Necessary Equipment

You need several basic pieces of equipment to run Windows. Here is a list of what you should have.

Type of Computer

You can run Windows on computers with the Intel 8086 or 8088 chip, such as the IBM PC and XT, but you may not be satisfied with the results, because many of Windows' fea-tures, including multitasking of non-Windows applications, will be unavailable. To take full advantage of Windows, you need a computer with the Intel 80286 or 80386 chip, such as the IBM PC AT and PS/2.

Amount of Memory

You need at least 640 KB of RAM to run Windows in Real mode, but performance will be poor with this little memory. For best performance, your computer should have at least

1 MB (640 KB of standard memory, plus 256 KB of extended memory) for Standard mode and 2 MB (640 KB standard memory, plus 1024 KB extended memory) for 386 Enhanced mode. All memory beyond 640 KB should be configured as extended memory. If you are uncertain of your computer's memory configuration, check your computer or memory-board documentation, or call your dealer. You can also buy special utilities that report on your computer's configuration.

Some extended memory managers are incompatible with the Windows memory manager. If you are running an in-compatible memory manager, Setup displays a dialog box asking whether you want to disable your extended memory manager. You probably want to answer Yes. You can always re-enable the memory manager later if disabling it causes problems with other software.

Operating System

You should be running MS-DOS or PC-DOS version 3.1 or later. If you have an earlier version of either DOS, you will have to obtain a new version from your software dealer.

Disk Drives

You need a hard disk drive with 6 to 8 MB of free storage space, and a high-density floppy-disk drive (for transferring programs from the installation disks). To find out how much free space is on your hard drive, type *dir* (for *directory*) at the DOS prompt, and press Enter. After listing the files and subdirectories in the active directory, DOS tells you how many bytes of disk space are free on the active drive.

Type of Display

Windows can work with many different monitors and graph-ics display adapters, but the graphical interface really comes into its own with a color EGA or VGA display. Setup provides a list of the display devices for which Windows has driver programs. If your display is not on the list, you can select a generic display driver—one that works with many types of displays—or you can consult your display manufacturer to see whether a driver has been developed specifically for your display and Windows.

Mouse

Just as you can run Windows on a PC XT, you can use Windows without a mouse. But as far as we are concerned, a mouse is not optional equipment, because using Windows from the keyboard is so cumbersome. If you don't have a mouse, you should buy one. Windows supports several different types of mice. Setup provides a list of the mice for which Windows has driver programs. If your mouse is not on the list, you can select a generic mouse driver—one that works with many types of mice—or you can consult your mouse manufacturer to see whether a driver has been developed specifically for your mouse and Windows.

Optional Windows Applications

To get the maximum benefit from the Windows environment, you should use applications written specifically for Windows, such as Microsoft Word for Windows, Microsoft Excel, Aldus Pagemaker, Corel Draw, and many others. Many software companies are currently in the process of writing Windows versions of their most popular software.

Optional Equipment

To use the Windows telecommunications program, Terminal, you need a modem. And to print your files, you need a printer. Windows supports many different types of printers. If your printer is not on Setup's list of supported devices, call your printer manufacturer to see whether a driver has been developed specifically for your printer and Windows.

What Setup Needs to Know

When you run Setup, the program makes "best guesses" concerning your computer's configuration. Often you can rely on Setup's guesses throughout the installation procedure, but you will need to verify the information. Here's what Setup will need to know:

- The directory to which it will copy the Windows programs. By default, Setup creates a WINDOWS directory on your C drive. If you want, you can specify a different directory and a different drive. Throughout this book, we assume you are running Windows from this directory.

- The type of computer you have.
- The type of monitor you have.
- The type of mouse you have—if any.
- The type of keyboard you have—standard or extended.
- The language you want to work in.
- The type of network you have—if any.
- The type of printer you have—if any—and what port it is connected to.

If you change your printer or any other piece of equipment after installing Windows, you can run the Setup program from within Windows to update the installation information.

Running Setup

Installation with Setup is really just a matter of reading the instructions at the bottom of each Setup screen and responding to prompts for disks. If you are unsure about a procedure while running Setup, press F1 for additional help. To start Setup:

1. Insert Disk 1 into your floppy drive. (We assume from now on that your floppy drive is Drive A.)
2. At the C prompt, type *A:*, and press Enter.
3. At the A prompt, type *setup*, and press Enter.

Halfway through the installation process, Setup will have copied enough of the Windows graphical environment files to your hard drive to continue the procedure from within Windows itself. You can tell when the switch to Windows occurs, because Setup starts displaying windows with scroll bars and dialog boxes with three-dimensional buttons. Toward the end of the installation process, Setup searches your hard drive for Windows applications, creates icons for them, and puts them in a set of windows. When Setup is finished, it displays a dialog box to tell you it has successfully installed Windows. Click the Reboot button to restart the computer.

While Setup is running, you can press the F3 key to exit the program. However, we don't recommend that you interrupt the program in this way, even if you give the wrong information, because Windows will not be properly installed and you will have to remove all the installed files and run Setup again. You are better off allowing Setup to completely install Windows and then running Setup again from within Windows to correct any mistakes.

If your computer crashes during the Setup process, irreparable harm may have been done to the Windows files already on your hard disk. Delete all the files in the WINDOWS directory, and run Setup again.

Appendix B
Notes about Networking

Because there are several different types of networks, generalizing about them can be difficult. In this appendix, we discuss basic procedures that will work on most types of networks. Check with your network system administrator for procedures that are specific to your network.

Installing Windows on a Networked Computer

On many networks, the system administrator installs Windows on a network server—a computer that stores resources and shares them with other computers on the network. You then install on your machine a copy of Windows that you obtain from the network server. You can access resources like Windows only if the system administrator has set your "network privileges" to permit access. If your network privileges permit access, you will be able to view the necessary server drives and directories in File Manager. If File Manager doesn't display these drives and directories, check with your network administrator about your access status.

Assuming that you can access Windows on the network server, this is the general procedure for installing a shared copy of Windows from the network server on your computer:

1. In File Manager, display the directory tree of the network server drive on which Windows is stored, by double-clicking its drive icon.

2. Double-click the WINDOWS folder to display its directory window.

3. Type *setup /n*, and press Enter.

Windows copies only the files you need to your computer, leaving most of the files on the server.

Logging On and Off

Logging on to a network usually involves entering a user name and password each time you need to access the network. To log on:

1. Click the Control Panel icon in Program Manager to open the Control Panel window. When the network software is loaded on your computer, the window displays a Network icon.

2. Double-click the Network icon to display the Network dialog box.

3. Choose Logon from the Account menu to display the Logon dialog box.

4. Type your user name in the Username text box. If your network requires that you enter a log-on password, type the password in the Password text box.

5. Click Logon. You can now use all the network resources available to you.

All networks are different, and logon procedures and restrictions differ for each. If you see a dialog box indicating a network error, contact your network system administrator.

After you have finished using the network, you need to log off. Some users simply turn off their computers without logging off, but logging off allows the network to disconnect gracefully and alerts any users who are accessing your machine. To log off:

1. Open Control Panel in Program Manager.

2. Double-click the Network icon.

3. Choose the Logoff command from the Account menu. You will be disconnected from the network and will no longer be able to use network applications. If you are using a copy of Windows that you installed from the server, you should now exit Windows.

4. Close the Network dialog box, close Control Panel, and choose Exit Windows from the File menu to quit Windows.

Points to Remember

When you are using Windows on a network, keep in mind the following:

- Always start the network software before you start Windows. Usually, the network software loads itself into your computer's memory. If you load Windows first, the network software may interfere with the way Windows handles memory.
- When creating icons in Program Manager for applications and documents that exist on the network server, always preface the file location with the appropriate server drive letter.
- You don't have to create Program Manager icons to run network programs. You can use File Manager or the Run command to start them.

Windows may behave differently on some networks than on others. If you are having difficulties, consult the Windows documentation or your network system administrator.

Index

Acknowledgments

Many thanks to Lori Sill and Christy Gersich at Microsoft; Peter Mayfield and the gang at CityRock Gym; Randy Fleming, Mark Ouimet, and the rest of the team at Publishers Group West; Ted Nace at Peachpit Press; Dorothy Smyk at New Harbinger Publications; and our many other friends in the publishing world who have been so helpful and supportive.

About Online Press

Founded in 1986, Online Press is a group of publishing professionals working to make the presentation and access of information manageable, efficient, accurate, and economical. In 1991 we began publishing our popular *Quick Course* computer-book series, offering streamlined instruction for today's busy professional. At Online Press, it is our goal to help computer users quickly learn what they need to know about today's most popular software programs to get their work done efficiently.

Cover design and photography by Tom Draper Design
Interior text design by Joyce Cox and Kjell Swedin
Text preparation and proofreading by Polly Urban
Graphics and layout by Kjell Swedin
Printed by Viking Press Inc.
Otabind® cover by Muscle Bound Bindery

Text composition by Online Press in Times Roman, with display type in Helvetica Narrow Bold, using Ventura Publisher and the Linotronic 300 laser imagesetter.